A Textbook of Healing

Previous publication

All This And Heaven Too – A Study in Past Lives (The Greater World Christian Spiritualist Association 1996)

A Textbook of Healing

Carol Brierly

Prometheus Press

Published 2004 by
Prometheus Press
c/o The Poetry Business
The Studio
Byram Arcade
Westgate
Huddersfield HD1 1ND

ISBN 1-869961-95-1

British Library Cataloguing-in-Publication Data
A catalogue record for this book is available from the British Library.

Printed by Antony Rowe Limited, Chippenham

Front cover photograph: 'Colorado Rainbow'
© Jason and Shi Garrett, Tyler, Texas

CONTENTS

Introduction 7

1. The Life Force 10
2. The Energy Centres Or Chakras 18
3. The Human Energy Field – The Aura 28
4. On Being A Healer 34
5. The Celestial Drainpipe 45
6. To Give A Healing 48
7. The Practice Of Meditation 52
8. Contacting The Sixth Sense 56
9. Practical Dowsing 61
10. Disease And Adverse Energies 67
11. Map Dowsing 81
12. Right And Left Brain Functions 86
13. Crystals And The Human Subtle Energy System 95
14. Flower And Gem Essences 104
15. The Eyes Have It 114
16. More Facts And Figures 121
17. Light And The Human Body 125
18. Colour In Healing 136
19. The Treatment Of Illness By Colour 142
20. The Language Of Colour 148
21. Sound 153
22. Natural Sound 160

Finale 171

Bibliography 174

Introduction

I was and am a dermatologist. I am also a healer. Perhaps I should have put that first because a dermatologist is an acquired profession and healing a natural way of life. In this book I am going to tell you about healing; about the basics that make a good healer and about the way that we can draw upon the energies of life, in essence the how and why of healing.

When I retired from the NHS, I opened a School of Healing and this is how this book came into being. It is based on the notes given to the students of my school. You will see that it is a mixture of experience and understanding both of health and of disease. We still have much to learn.

It is about twenty years since I gave my first healing – and here almost immediately I am wrong, for the healing was not of my doing, not really. Neither was the healing from a being whom we call God. Who then, or possibly what, was the healer? My patient healed herself. That is not to say that God had no hand in this, of course He had. But in the terms of this world, the lady healed herself.

Let me tell you how this happened. One day, at the end of the Outpatient Clinic, one of the appointment clerks asked to see me. Her mother, she said, was dying. She had had a brain tumour which had been only partially removed. As a result of the operation she had lost the use of both legs and had almost complete loss of movement in her right arm. The tumour was still growing and she could now hardly see. Her elderly husband was finding it almost impossible to cope. Would I, my friend said, tell her that she must now go into care.

All my instincts were against this but I promised to go to see the lady.

Might I first try the effects of healing?

And so, week after week, I visited her, pouring healing into her body in every way that I knew. Nothing happened except that we became friends. I must tell her, I thought, about going into the hostel. I could put it off no longer. I would tell her on my next visit.

But I never told her. I meant to, but as I approached the door, I could see her through the window. She was watching TV. This blind old woman was watching TV and she was doubled up with laughter. It was indeed a very funny programme. She could see! Not very well, of course, but sufficiently well to enjoy the programme.

Over the weeks her sight improved. She began to read. Life seemed worth living again. A little grandson had been born. She was looking forward to seeing the baby.

The next thing was, I caught her knitting. Something for the baby, she said. The partially paralysed arm had come to life. From then onwards there was no stopping her. Her legs were of little use to her but she hopped around with a zimmer, started to do the cooking, a little housework and together she and her husband and a wheelchair went off in the car. They were like children, contented and happy. I left them at this point.

Seven years later I had a phone call. My first patient was dying. She was unconscious but the family wished to say goodbye. Could I bring her back into consciousness so that they could do so? What, me? How could I possibly do that!

I went. The whole family was there, children and grandchildren and, I suspect, the neighbours also. I banished the lot from the bedside and when we were alone together, I began to talk to her and then I put my hands on her head. She opened her eyes and with a little help she sat up. She said goodbye to her children, smiled at them, smiled at me and died.

I felt profoundly humbled.

1
The Life Force

A life force is the one thing which we all share and which we have in common with everything in this world and indeed with everything within our Universe. Life in its essence is intangible, unseeable, unsmellable and impossible to analyse. It is present in all things, in rocks, plants, animals, although in some of its forms, for example in rocks, it is unmanifest to the human view. In what we like to term 'living things', life is manifest, causing dynamic change, moving and flowing, ever-present.

The energy that keeps us alive has to be, if we accept it as present, the essence of everything: the force that holds the parts of an atom together, the power that makes a small seed grow, that keeps a single cell alive and functioning, the attractive power of gravity and magnetism and the power of consciousness. This same life force manifests itself in different ways: in plants so that we have the different species and properties in one group as opposed to another; in animals where again we see different species; and in man with his many races and personalities.

The life force continually brings about a state of balance within our body, and in health, a state of harmony. It is responsible for every activity taking place within us: the beating of the heart, the conduction of nerves, regulation of breathing, of temperature, enzyme activity, glandular function and much much more. A higher force than the brain is necessary for control. This energy is the central harmonising and balancing influence within us.

We have come to believe that the brain is the ultimate controller of the body, but this is not so. The brain acts much as a computer will act in control of a business. It stores information and activates different channels, which in turn will affect bodily function and maintain equilibrium. In this way it regulates and maintains the body; but a higher force, the life force, is necessary for life. When we die the brain is still intact, the body may still be able to function, but something vital to life has been withdrawn. This is the life force.

Everything has a surrounding field of energy whether it is animate or inanimate, whether it is alive or dead. In dead things the field changes as the energies generated from the breakdown of tissue alter. There is never wasted energy, only energy in another form which can be released for re-use.

Each energy field affects the fields adjacent to it. A field of energy is composed of vibrational energies of one type or another, which travel in wave form.

Each part of what we call a living organism, i.e. plants, invertebrates, insects, birds and mammals, has its own separate field of energy and the shape and size of this and its constituent parts is controlled by a limiting membrane. If the energy field becomes distorted in any way, the shape and constitution of the part is altered; and we think in this context of disease such as the formation of tumours, or conditions such as cirrhosis of the liver.

Energies travel in wave form and are vibrational, the different energies having different rates of vibration. The energies of colour, for example, have a range of vibration rates in the electromagnetic spectrum. The workings of the animal kingdom are also governed by electromagnetic energies. Sound has different vibrational frequencies to light and the higher energies such as ultraviolet light and X-rays have even higher frequencies. The highest energy which we know as spiritual energy has vibrational frequencies so high that we are unable to measure them but we know that they are there because we are able to feel them and observe their effects.

The human body is operated by electromagnetic energies. Each part of the body has its own field of energy: liver, lungs, skin, muscles, brain. Each field has a range of distinctive vibrations, and as one field can affect another, each part within our body can affect, not only its immediate neighbour, but the body as a whole. This is one reason why an illness is not confined to one organ only but affects those which have similar vibrations to its own. If the heart is affected then the whole circulatory system is affected. If conduction in a nerve is altered, paralysis of the part supplied may follow. That this appears to be carried out by physical or chemical means in no way alters this concept, for blood vessels and nerves are also composed of vibrational fields. We can pick up the different vibrations from the body with sensitive instruments and get wave tracings from the brain, the heart and the muscles respectively, and we can tell whether the vibration is abnormal or whether it is the normal vibration for the part. In the same way we can pick up the outer field energies of the body and tell whether they are normal, or whether there is any abnormality.

One field alters another field and this is true not only of the physical fields. Emotional energies such as fear or anger may produce alteration within the affected person and can produce the same emotions in another person. Panic can spread in the same way. Anger can affect the physical side of both ourselves and others. Fear can act similarly and we find an increased heartbeat, or we may have diarrhoea due to stimulation of the muscle of the gut. So we can understand that an abnormal vibrational energy wave can alter a normal one. The reverse is also true; a normal vibrational wave or a wave of a higher multiplication of that wave which harmonises with it can restore the normal to the abnormal. It works both ways.

The air around us is filled with waves of energy – all vibrations of one sort or another. We know that sound waves are there because we can record them instrumentally. We can also record heat vibrations, high frequency radio and television, low frequency earth energy waves and so on. There are also waves of such high frequency that we are unable to measure them. All these energies can pass into and through the body and they crisscross within us. Where they cross the energies are altered, increased or decreased.

Within the body where there is a concentration of the incoming energy we have the formation of energy centres. Here it is more easy for energies to move in or out. Depending on the amount of energy crossing at any one point they are classed as major or minor centres. The minor centres are the acupuncture points. The seven major centres are situated along the spine and they may be contacted on other parts of the body, front or back. They are termed the chakras and we will discuss them further in the next chapter. Minor centres are also found on the palms, the soles of the feet and many other places. All centres, major or minor, are important as a means of transmitting and receiving energy.

Some energies out side the body are potentially destructive and we must if possible reduce them to the amount that the body can take without injury to the tissues. Conversely if we wish to destroy certain tissues, for example a malignant tumour, we must be sure that the right amount of irradiation is given exactly to the area affected. Some energies have so low a vibration that a summation of the individual amounts is necessary before they have a measurable effect. This type of energy may be used in medical treatment, for example in the treatment of the skin, a maximum of 1500 roentgen units may be given during a lifetime and this is carried out in divided doses.

To sum up

The life force within the world and within us is composed of radiating fields of energy, each with its own frequency and amplitude, which in turn is dependent upon the level of substance through which it travels. Physical energy fields are very dense, emotional fields less dense and so on. We are living in a web of energies which is spread throughout the cosmos, throughout the earth and through our own bodies, penetrating to the innermost cell.

Ideally we should have harmony within and between these energy fields and within the energy fields of our own bodies.

We do not have this.

When one energy field is altered, the harmony of the whole is altered and in some cases disrupted. This happens not only in bodily events but in world events also, and we can see the effects of this in wars and also in the destruction of the environment by man. It happens also in the balance of man with his surroundings and of man with his fellow man. It is within the interaction of the fields around us that we live and have our being.

There are many simple ways of demonstrating our own energy flow. One of the simplest is to sit in front of an electric fire in a darkened room. Holding the palms of the hands in the same plane as the fire, fingers touching, draw the hands apart. Energy lines will flow from the fingers of one hand to the other. Raise one hand slightly and the angle of the flow will alter.

Another way is to roll a piece of paper about 10 by 30 cms. and glue the bottom to the top end (see Fig.1, p.16). You now have a cylinder [step two].

Fasten a sliver of wood or paper across the top diameter of the cylinder.

Balance the centre of this on a long needle (stuck into a cork) and the whole on top of a block of wood or a tin [step four]. When balanced and steady point one finger tangentially at the balanced cylinder which will then rotate as the energy streams off the finger onto the cylinder.

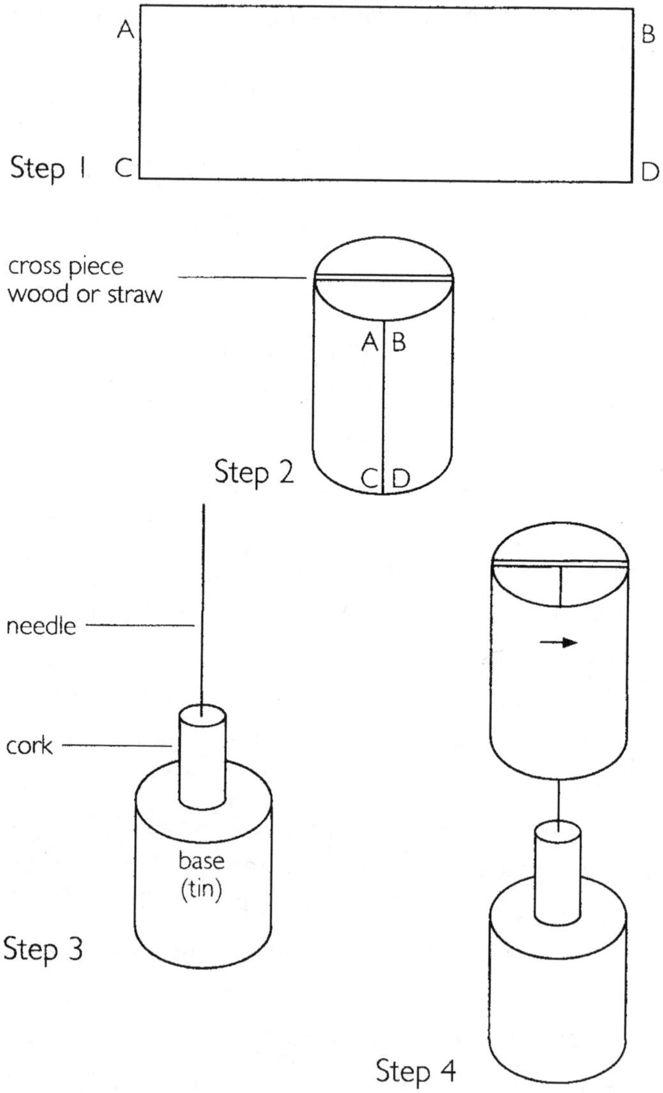

Demonstrating energy flow

Kirlian photography will also demonstrate energy flow not only from the hands but from seeds, leaves and crystals, showing that it is not only living plants and animals which possess energy fields, but that so-called inanimate objects have energy fields also. The Kirlian camera was developed just before World War Two in 1939 by Semyon Davidovitch Kirlian. He was working on an electrical apparatus when he received a severe shock. He stopped work and went home. His wife Valentina asked him to help with some photographic work.

Kirlian photograph of the hand showing the surrounding etheric field

Semyon took a new film and handed it to his wife who developed it. The negatives showed distinct colours of blue and yellow extending outside the contours of his hand. How this phenomenon arises is still a subject of much debate but that it shows electromagnetic energy produced by the body is not disputed. It is for us to decide its function and its value.

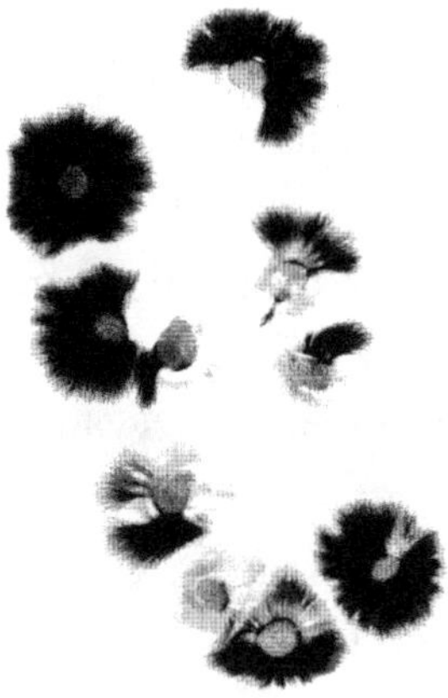

Kirlian photograph of the finger tips showing the etheric field

2
The Energy Centres Or Chakras

The chakras are specialised energy centres which connect us to the higher energy levels of the universe. They take in and process energy of a high vibrational nature so that it may be properly assimilated and used to transform the physical body. Each of the major chakras is connected to a major nerve plexus and glandular centre within the endocrine system of the body.

Each major chakra is also associated with a particular physiological system. Thus the heart chakra is associated with the whole of the circulatory system and also the physical ear; the throat chakra with the throat and thyroid gland.

The chakras help to regulate the flow of vital energy into the organs of the body. This brings strength and balance into these areas. Imbalance or abnormal chakra function can create weakness in the area of the body which it serves and may influence the manifestation of illness within that area.

Chakras bring a type of subtle nutritive energy to specific parts of the body. These higher vibrational energies are vitally necessary for the growth and maintenance of life. The subtle energy currents help in promoting stability and organisation within the energy field immediately surrounding the physical body. This is known as the etheric field and it is here that energy changes are manifest before they enter and become manifest at the physical cellular level.

Currents of energy are taken into the body through a stream entering the crown chakra which is at the top of the head. The chakras are closely linked to the spinal cord and to the nerve ganglia along the central axis of the body. From the crown chakra the energy flows to the lower chakras which distribute the subtle currents to the appropriate organs and body parts. Each chakra is associated with a range of different vibrational frequencies which are necessary to the parts of the body which it serves.

The chakras also relate to various aspects of consciousness, especially the emotions which may affect the flow of energy through these centres. When the emotional field in any area is disturbed, the flow of subtle energy through the chakra supplying that area is altered and results in altered function. Emotion may thus affect the heart, causing increased heartbeat, or the gut, the eyes or nasal glands with varying results. Each of the seven major chakras has a particular emotional and spiritual issue which affects its proper functioning. When someone has unresolved emotional issues in any one of these areas, the chakra may become dysfunctional. The flow of nutritive subtle energy supplied through the impaired chakra diminishes and the associated body region, the organs and glands may be thrown into cellular imbalance. If the chakra blockage persists, disease of these areas may eventually occur. Altered subtle energy flow through the various chakras is one mechanism by which chronic stress can affect the physical body.

Chakras are associated with different emotional and spiritual issues in the development of our consciousness; we should also not underestimate their importance when it comes to our physical well-being.

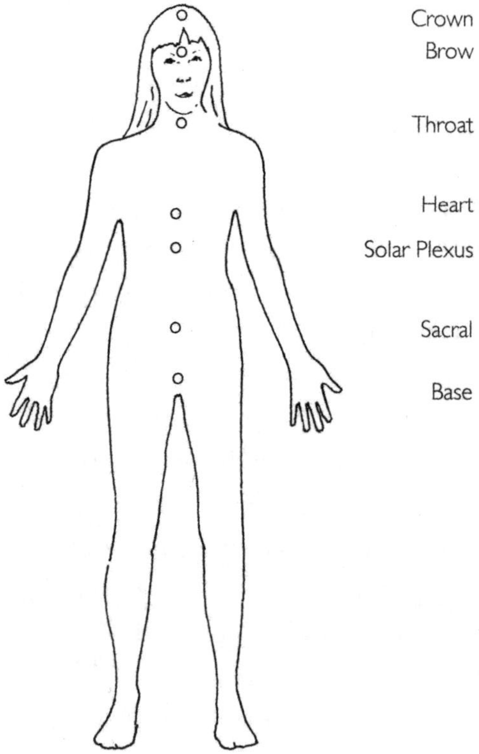

Chakra points

Crown Chakra. Situated just above the top of the head is the crown chakra. This higher vibrational centre is associated with the higher levels of consciousness. It is tied on the physical level to the activity of the cerebral cortex and to the functioning of the central nervous system. Activation of this chakra influences the synchronisation of the right and left cerebral hemispheres with the pineal gland. The chakra does not open until the body, mind and spirit are fully balanced. Abnormalities of flow may show as cerebral dysfunction including psychoses.

Third Eye. The brow centre is known as the third eye and is associated with the pineal gland. This gland is situated at the back of the skull and shows rudimentary eye tissue. In reptiles the pineal gland is still associated with sight. When the crown centre becomes active the brow centre has an energy polarity between the pineal and the pituitary glands. When the crown centre is not active the brow centre is associated with the pituitary gland and the medulla oblongata.

The third eye is the seat of intuition and is involved in clairvoyance. Third eye vision when the chakra is fully open gives acute awareness and a greater insight. In the majority of people the third eye is not active but it is found that it develops gradually through meditative practice. Third eye vision focuses awareness and brings clearer insight. Physically this charka also serves the spinal cord, the eyes, the ears and the sinuses. Energy blockages at the level of this chakra may show as sinus problems, cataracts and major endocrine disturbances. This last is because of its influence over the pituitary gland.

Throat Chakra. The throat chakra influences all the structures in the neck, the thyroid and parathyroid glands, the mouth, the vocal cords and the trachea as well as the cervical vertebrae. There is also an association between the throat chakra and the vagus nerve which travels through the neck to innervate the heart, the lungs and the organs of the abdomen.

The thyroid and the parathyroid glands are both endocrine glands. The hormone from the thyroid gland, thyroxin, regulates the metabolic activity of the cells of the body and the thyroid also produces calcitonin which affects calcium and bone activity.

The parathyroid gland also regulates calcium metabolism. Because the throat chakra energises both glands it affects general skeletal activity.

The throat chakra is important in communication and when fully developed it functions in clairaudience. Dysfunction of this centre may present as difficulty in communication, difficulty in expressing oneself in front of other people.

This chakra is the centre of higher creative ability, of word and song. Where there is a blockage or too little energy passing through this centre, the person may be unable to express himself creatively and he may not realise this. Abnormalities of energy involve those parts which are dependent upon this centre. Too little may lead to degenerative disease or to hypothyroidism, too much to inflammation of the area, to an overactive thyroid or to tumours of the larynx.

Heart Chakra. The heart chakra is concerned with the expression of love, both self love and love of other people. We talk of an open heart and this is essential for true love. There are many forms of love but the highest of these is unconditional love for others.

Abnormalities of the heart centre may show as difficulties

in learning how to love and may follow a lack of nurturing as a child or in early adult life. To be able to express love one must have experienced love, and many children have not done so.

Malfunction of the heart chakra may affect the physical ear. This is a developmental anomaly. As the heart develops it moves downwards from the shoulder area to the chest, but its relationships with its former associates persists, and the ear is one of these. The heart chakra supplies energy to the whole circulatory system as well as the bronchi, lungs and breasts. The importance of this centre cannot be overstressed. Imbalance can not only affect the structure of the heart and manifest as coronary disease but can lead to bacterial and viral illness and cancers of the area supplied. It can affect the blood flow through the heart and may be the precursor of a stroke. Other diseases such as asthma can be the result of unbalanced heart energy creating a spasm of the bronchial tubes.

The heart chakra occupies a position between the higher spiritual energies and the lower earth energies. Because it is closely tied to the expression of love and compassion it is an important centre of nurture. As the centre becomes more open these spiritual energies increase and the emotions bind people in loving relationships. The development of compassion and love for the world is the first stage in the opening of the heart chakra and the development of higher potential.

The Thymus. Although this centre is generally not considered to be one of the main chakra centres it does nevertheless play a very important role in the regulation of the immune response. The thymus is primarily functional throughout childhood when T-lymphocytes are pre-programmed for special immunological capabilities. This takes place within the thymus gland. In addition the thymus gland also produces hormones called thymosins which enhance the activity of T-lymphocytes and enable the individual to fight off disease. More will be said about this later.

There is a strong association between depression and grief and suppression of immune function. An example of this is the frequent development of carcinoma 12–18 months after the death of a member of the family. Patients with immune suppression of any sort are at a greater risk of malignancy. The autoimmune diseases include rheumatoid arthritis, lupus vulgaris, myaesthenia gravis, multiple sclerosis, Hashimoto's thyroiditis, adrenal failure and primary ovarian failure.

The predisposition to illness appears to relate to emotional imbalances of the heart centre and love ability. Blockages in the chakra may arise from inability to express love but it is more often a lack of self love, persistent negativity and loss of self worth. Often many of the chakras are not functioning normally. Blockage of energy flow in one chakra may result in too much energy entering the centre below. If there is a block or partial block at the heart chakra, more energy may be pouring through the solar plexus. The energy generated in the base or root chakra tends to rise up the spine to the crown centre and supply the chakras in ascending order as it rises. If the chakras are blocked or partially blocked there is likely to be congestion and overflow of energy in the lower centres. An individual may have multiple emotional blockages, and these are often issues which have not been dealt with adequately by that person.

Many emotional and spiritual difficulties lie in this area. They are problems which have not been dealt with adequately by people with dysfunction at the level of the heart chakra. They concern the opposing emotions of grief and joy.

Imbalance in the heart chakra is often shown in those people who have lives which are lonely and filled with grief and sadness. They find it difficult to show love. The world seems against them. Terminal illness in members of their family brings feelings of guilt. They are unable to feel and to show joy to others. All this, and more, blocks the energy flow through the heart chakra and this at a later stage can show as dysfunction at the level of the thymus.

Because the thymus can affect many types of disease-fighting cells, abnormal thymus function can create a general weakness in immune defences. Bacterial and viral infections can invade. The production of T-lymphocytes by the gland is all important for cellular immunity. There are several types of T-cells. Some release cytotoxic substances which destroy invading cells. Other cells, called Helper cells stimulate the formation of antibodies, whilst cells called Suppressor cells prevent reactions which might damage the body. Sometimes a whole system breaks down and the body loses its immunity to its own tissues. This is followed by autoimmune diseases of which there are many. Diseases that result from autoimmunity include rheumatic fever, lupus erythematosus, adrenal failure and primary ovarian failure. Autoimmune adrenal failure may be associated also with dysfunction in the heart chakra, and similarly primary ovarian failure with subtle energy blockage in the heart chakra and in the sacral chakra.

The Solar Plexus Chakra is a common site for energy blockage.

The solar plexus supplies nutritive subtle energy to most of the organs of digestion except to the intestines. This centre is linked to issues of personal power, of control over life.

It relates to how people see themselves in relation to other people. So-called 'victim-conscious' people often show imbalance in the solar plexus.

Stress can manifest as illness following energy blockage in this area. Domination, anger, and abuse of others can be associated with abnormal function of the solar plexus. Often the anger is directed to others as a result of an inner feeling of powerlessness and is discharged on people who are innocent of offence. There seems to be a preoccupation with dominance and control of others. For this reason people may be alternatively assertive and aggressive, or cowardly and submissive in their attitudes to people around them. Some people seem to alternate between the two extremes.

Imbalance can affect any of the digestive organs which are affected by this chakra. Ulcers are common. Conditions which are linked to more than one centre can occur. For example the adrenal glands are linked to the solar plexus chakra and in addition are also linked to the basal or root chakra. Blockages at either centre may lead to disease and degeneration of the adrenals with subsequent fatigue and weakness. Another disease which is linked with the solar plexus is diabetes. Diabetics tend to feel a loss of personal power.

The Sacral Chakra is associated with sexuality, with the gonads and reproductive organs and also with the bladder, small intestines and the lumbar region as a whole. The flow of energy through this centre is connected with the higher centres and with creativity, but focus is usually on relationships for their sexual and sensual effects. Physically the energies relate to the hormonal control of sex.

The colon and the urinary tract are also under the influence of this chakra.

The types of illness associated with the sacral chakra are obvious – cervical and uterine cancer, irritable bowels, bladder tumours, malabsorption and sexual dysfunction. This is the lower centre of physical creativity and as such is intimately associated with the throat chakra.

The Base or *Root Chakra* is the lowest of the centres connected with the human body. It determines the degree that we are connected to the earth or that we are grounded in our activities. On a psychological level the root chakra is related to the basic survival instincts of fight or flight. Hence the association with the adrenal glands and adrenaline. It is the storehouse for the natural and powerful energy which we know as the kundalini. This energy has the power to activate and align all of the major chakras with the higher centres and to bring in illumination and spiritual enlightenment to the body as the chakras unfold. The energy develops naturally over a period of time. Should the release be sudden or enforced it can in a sense 'blow' the circuitry of the energy centres and channels, causing all sorts of serious imbalance.

3
The Human Energy Field – The Aura

The human energy field, the Aura, is the manifestation of that part of the universal energy field that is involved in life. It is a luminous area which surrounds and interpenetrates the human body. Within this area of luminosity, different levels can be seen. Each is given off by succeeding layers of body, emotions and mind and each is composed of successively finer vibrations.

The first layer can be seen about half to one inch outside the physical body. It is perhaps the most easy to see, because it appears denser than the other layers. This field is concerned with autonomic and automatic functioning and also with physical sensation. It is called the *etheric body*. The etheric body is composed of fine energy lines and interpenetrates the physical body (as do all the other fields). It has the same anatomical structure as the physical body including all the parts and organs, and may be considered to be the template for the physical body in that this vital energy field precedes the physical body which is superimposed upon it. The etheric body pulsates and the rate of pulsation is about 15-20 cycles per minute. The colour varies from grey to light blue, the blue being seen by people who are more sensitive.

The second layer is concerned with the *emotional* aspects of the human being. It stands out about one to three inches from the physical body. Because it is associated with the emotions it seems more fluid than the etheric body and it does not replicate the physical body. Instead it is composed of moving blobs of colour which vary all the time and may show as brilliant clear hues or dull muddy ones, depending as they do on the level of emotion.

The third layer, the *mental body*, extends even further out and can be seen as a bright yellow area. It is composed of even finer matter and is highly structured. Thought forms can be seen as blobs of varying brightness and definition. Thoughts and emotions are often mixed and emotional colours may be seen frequently.

There are seven energy layers in the aura. The lower three layers are usually the only ones that we can see. They metabolise the energies which are related to the physical body. The three highest levels which are related to the three highest chakras metabolise the spiritual energies of man. The fourth level is related to the level of the heart and is concerned with transformation of spiritual energies into physical energies and vice versa.

This fourth layer of the aura is called the *astral layer*, because it scintillates with light and colour, mainly with the rose colour of love. It extends up to a foot beyond the physical body. Within this area can be seen people or beings who exist but have no physical body. This is a layer of reality which is hidden from most of us and can only be seen by people whose perception is open.

Each layer above the third layer has its own reality with apparent beings and forms: these inhabit worlds which we normally only experience during sleep. We cannot normally see them except in the sleep state but occasionally we seem to be able to see these when awake. For example when two people are in love, one may be able to see arcs of rose coloured light between their heart chakras. Or perhaps blobs of colour flash between two people. I am never quite sure at which level this takes place. Although perhaps it sounds almost too silly to be true, I once saw a hat! It happened in this way. I was at a meeting of a Society and we were all having tea. It was a lovely day and the windows of the big room were open. A woman walked in through one of the French windows. She had a most extraordinary hat on her head.

It was black with what appeared to be little snakes writhing around the brim. And it seemed to be on fire. When I next saw her the hat was nowhere to be seen. I crossed the room to see if she had put it down somewhere but there was nothing. And then I got the biggest shock of my life. I saw the hat materialise on her head, the snakes, the flames, everything. Later I learned that she had been passed over for an important job in the Society and could hardly conceal her jealousy when she saw her rival.

Strange things happen and it is difficult to know why they happen or from what level of the aura they arise. Quite often one can see light surrounding people, often a speaker on a platform, but not always so. Once at a concert of chamber music I saw the first violinist surrounded by radiant light. He was playing brilliantly, and it seemed that he was in love with his violin, or perhaps his violin was in love with him. It did not matter. Almost everyone in the audience saw his halo of light. These are mind-blowing experiences when they happen, never to be forgotten.

The fifth layer of the aura is the *etheric template*, the blueprint for the etheric layer which is the grid structure on which the physical body is formed. This extends out widely but it is rarely seen.

Next is the emotional layer of the spiritual plane. Here we experience ecstasy and we may reach this level in various ways, including through the practice of meditation. It is an area of unconditional love. When the channel to the heart chakra is open the spiritual love for humanity flows freely.

This is the sixth layer and it is called the *celestial body*. It extends to roughly three feet from the body and seems to be composed of radiating beams of shimmering light in opalescent pastel colours.

The next or outermost layer is called the *ketheric template* of the causal body, and it may be as much as three and a half feet wide. When our consciousness is centred in this area we are said to be one with the Creator. It appears to be a highly complex area and 'shimmers with gold'. This level contains the main power current which runs up and down the spine and nourishes the whole body. It carries energies through the roots of each chakra and connects the energies that are taken in through the chakra.

Two other levels lie outside the bodily fields and these are associated with the eighth and ninth chakras which are situated above the head. Sadly we are unable to see them.

How To Look At The Aura

Most people can see the aura but many people dismiss what they see. To look for something is not necessarily to see it.

Initially the aura seems indistinct and hazy but as we develop the higher aspects of our being and our higher senses it becomes clearer. For some people it has always been clear and they are the lucky ones. They may have spent many lives developing the ability to see. For others, a hazy outline is all that there is and sometimes not even that.

To see the aura, one must first have quiet within oneself. Our subject should, preferably have a plain wall behind them because this shows the colour more effectively. I find that light grey or beige walls are best for this.

When looking, try not to focus upon the other person. Try to defocus. Look beyond your subject. Start by looking at the area close to the head. You will see a lighter surround, about half an inch higher. This is the etheric body – a little bigger than the body, rather as a dress pattern is a little bigger than the finished garment to allow for seams. The colour of the etheric surround is normally a light grey-blue. It is three-dimensional and it interpenetrates the physical body.

Next, look outwards from the etheric: six to nine inches. There seems to be an edge here where the haziness ends. You are looking at the mental body. The edge is yellow, a sort of mandarin yellow and it is often very definite. Between this and the etheric is a rather nebulous swirling area – like a loose sort of mist – shot through with flashes of colour, pinks, blues, rather like a lovely sunset. At first you will see very little but as you continue to look you may see more. Make your friend angry and you may see red or vivid orange flashes. These are the emotions, little bursts of irritation (red, black), little loving thoughts (pink), and so on. Sometimes the colours look like symbols and may tell you something else about your friend; remember the lady with the hat!

One warning, don't spend all your time looking at auras or you will lose your friends. No one likes to feel that you are seeing what they wish to hide!

Lower thought and emotion are often mixed together but higher thought is in a higher vibratory dimension. This is not very marked in most of us but in the higher intellectual and the thinker it may be very clear.

People who are evolving see different things. If you are interested in healing you may be able to see pain in the etheric. Usually red, it stands out in a streak of colour along the outer edge of the part affected. Inflammation can also be seen on the etheric as a dull diffuse red. Occasionally one can see a grey dullness in this area over the site of a, usually malignant, tumour. This may be evident before the tumour is apparent within the body, suggesting perhaps that illness begins in this area and appears later in the physical body. I suggest that you keep these observations to yourself; it is not necessary for your friend to know and it is only too easy to be wrong.

One last word – don't give up, don't stop looking. At the beginning the aura is very difficult for most people to see. But keep on looking and don't try too hard to see because this defeats the object. One day you will be surprised!

4
On Being A Healer

The ability to heal is not a sudden miracle, although it may often appear to be so. The intuitive and receptive qualities necessary to the healer depend largely on self knowledge and a high level of awareness. It has taken many years and many lifetimes to develop. To heal others it is necessary first to heal yourself. The two are closely related. To be a pure and effective channel for the healing energies requires both dedication and understanding; an understanding not only of the patient and his immediate problem but an understanding of humanity as a whole and ourselves in particular.

What do we, or our patients, expect from healing?

The power of healing has no limits and the change may be instantaneous and complete, or slow, or partial. To expect an instant result often leads to disappointment and misunderstanding. Moreover an instant cure, whilst flattering for the healer, is not always acceptable to the patient or the relatives. A slow and continuous improvement is usually preferable. In this way, both patient and relatives can adjust to the changing situation and prepare for a return to total health. To understand this, imagine that you have been blind and can suddenly see again. You would of course be overjoyed. You would want to tell everyone about it. It takes some time to adjust to a situation like this and so perhaps you wait for an hour or two or a day before you tell them. They are delighted for you, of course, but the delight may be tempered with suspicion. Have you been hiding the truth from them for a longer time, allowing them perhaps to help you when help was not needed, to guide you, to do your shopping? Have they perhaps been taken for a ride? And now comes the point where you must inform your doctor. He does not believe in miracles except miracles of medicine and surgery and clearly neither of these has happened. And in his own mind he is running through the text book to find conditions which can produce temporary blindness, such as MS, such as … He asks pertinent questions and seems irritated by your answers. Not an altogether happy interview, although ultimately and perhaps rather grudgingly he admits that your sight is perfect. Other complications arise: the DSS and your supplementary pension. They also do not believe in miracles and they suspect fraud. And so it goes on – summons perhaps for obtaining money fraudulently. Tax problems on increased income. The mind boggles. Perhaps it would have been better to have remained blind or at least to have recovered your sight more gradually.

Healing occurs at all levels. A person who is healed at the physical level may not be able to sustain that cure because other levels are not sufficiently developed and behaviour patterns and patterns of thought have not altered. In this situation the healing can only be temporary. Over a period of time, the condition will recur.

There seem to be certain situations where the patient is not ready to be cured and where healing at a physical level appears to be a failure.

The reasons for illness are not always fully understood. The disease seems still to be necessary to the patient. Moreover an emotional or mental state may produce physical symptoms or even disease itself. I remember a patient whom I used to see every Saturday morning. This enormous and very healthy woman would lumber up the path, always at the end of the surgery. She had, she said, cancer. I cannot count the number of times that I examined her. My partner examined her. We did tests. There was nothing that we could find. We sent her to specialists. They also could find no abnormality. Then one day, as I was working at the local hospital, one of the nurses told me that she had been admitted to the ward with a diagnosis of cancer. I had seen her in the previous week and she had seemed in the best of health. I went up to the ward to find that she was already dead. A postmortem on the following day showed cancer deposits in practically every organ that one could think of. I am convinced to this day that her thoughts and fears had produced reality. This was my first experience of a disease produced in this way.

Behaviour, mismanagement of our lives, fear, uncertainty, and above all stress can produce illness. Why? How? Is it there so that we may learn from it? Illness seems often to be a resting period when other sides of our personalities are given time to develop. My own illness, spread over many many years has taught me more than I could possibly say. I have learned to bear pain, to have courage, to be patient and above all I have learned what it is to be ill; understanding the feelings of others, the fears and the hopes – often to be dashed to the ground. I am eternally grateful to my bones, even though they have left me with a legacy of discomfort and physical limitation. Disease, it is said, may be caused by our behaviour and mismanagement in past lives. I have no means of knowing this in myself. I suspect it sometimes in others. In a state of hypnotic regression one can sometimes take people back to the life where the illness or the condition first started. Many of these conditions are not in past lives but start before or at the moment of birth. Lack of bonding with one's mother may follow rejection of the child or even the removal by the nursing staff of the baby immediately after birth. Sometimes after a caesarian operation, the baby is also removed immediately. I remember one girl under hypnosis saying as she was carried out to a cot, 'She's not looking at me. Her eyes are shut. My Mummy's not looking at me.' Her mother was of course anaesthetised and no bonding took place. This was a problem to the girl in later life.

Although it may seem strange, we must also remember that some people do not want to become well. Compensation claims cloud the issue, but there are also those who need an illness to lift them out of an impossible situation or in whom the attention and care that illness brings may satisfy a real need within the patient.

Two instances of this come to mind. The first was an old nun of 86 years – one of the Little Sisters of the Poor. Their convent was a cold gaunt Victorian structure, where these dedicated women lived and gave their lives to the surrounding poor. They also were pathetically poor.

It was one of the worst winters that I have ever known. I

was in Leeds at the time having just qualified in medicine. The little nun was admitted, half starved and bitterly cold, with a huge ulcer on her leg. To her, it must have seemed like Heaven. She was in a ward, warm, comfortable with good food and privacy. She was allowed to draw her curtains round her bed, she was after all religious and a sweet saintly woman. She started to get better – and fatter. The day came when the ulcer had healed. We arranged for her to go home. But at the last minute the ulcer broke down and we decided to keep her for a further week. Outside the weather was still appalling with sub zero temperatures.

On the following week as we did our ward round, our consultant, who was a tiny vital little man, tiptoed down the ward and yanked back the curtains around her bed. There sat our nun, a huge nappy pin in her hand, picking away at her ulcer for dear life. Poor little soul, who could blame her and who in the circumstances would want to get better?

Some of us need an illness. Another elderly lady whose sister was bedridden was in her late seventies and attended outpatients with a mild eczema of her hands, which cleared rapidly on treatment. It recurred, cleared, and recurred again. There was clearly something wrong. Then, on questioning, it all came out. She spent her day looking after her sister, who was bedridden, climbing the stairs with meals, cups of tea, letters, papers. She made tea for visitors, washed up the cups. And she was tired out, deflated. 'If only', she said in tears, 'they would do something for me. If only they would say to me, 'and how are you, Emma, how are your hands? Let me help you wash those dishes.' And I would say that I was attending the Infirmary for treatment. So we kept her on our outpatients list. Sometimes we bandaged her hands or altered her medicine so that she could hold up her head among her neighbours. Yes, some people do not want to get better. The illness satisfies their need.

Every healer should follow a code of behaviour, a code of good manners between not only healer and the patient but between healer and his fellow workers. Every profession has its ethics and rules of conduct, which its members follow.

One of the first great schools of healing was that of Aesculapius on the Island of Cos. Here Hippocrates lived and taught. The Hippocratic Oath which binds all members of the medical profession, healers and doctors alike, runs as follows:

> You will lead your lives and practise your art in uprightness and honour; that into whatever house you shall enter, it shall be for the good of the sick to the utmost of your power, you holding yourself far aloof from wrong, from corruption, and from the temptation of others to vice …

The healer then, acts only in the patient's interests and if he feels that a particular line of treatment is not in the interest of the patient, he refrains from using it. Even though he may see that a patient is in need of healing the healer never forces his attention on that person. It is necessary for the patient to take the first step and for them or their relative to ask for help. A healer or doctor never takes patients from a colleague unless asked to do so by that colleague. Occasionally the patient may wish to change to another healer and he should have the good manners to tell his previous carer.

A healer or doctor should never boast about his skills to the detriment of others, never openly criticise another's methods.

We all fall down on this, healers and doctors alike. We criticise our colleagues whilst at the same time suggesting that we are better. Our methods of treatment are not always in the interests of our patients. Sometimes we wish to experiment with a particular patient. I remember a local doctor – an elderly lady who when she visited would sit down at the piano and sing a hymn. Then she would say, 'It'll be all right now', and go home. Apocrophal – perhaps!

It happens among healers too – with the best of intentions.

It is advisable for a lay healer, with very little medical knowledge of his own, to work as far as possible with the knowledge and assistance of the medical profession. Ideally there should be a partnership of skills. That this is not always possible reflects on both layman and doctor. Many doctors resent what they see as intrusion by the layman into matters of which he knows next to nothing. The layman on the other hand sees the doctor as arrogant and blind, hiding behind his so-called standards. Neither understands the other. Neither is willing to learn. All too often both are wrong.

There is, or there used to be, considerable opposition from healers to understand anything about the human body. They feel that some knowledge of anatomy and physiology is not necessary. Healing comes from God and God knows where to send it. But it is important to know what we are doing and why we are doing it and to understand a little about disease and its effects and when and where to treat. For those who attend healing courses today an understanding of anatomy and physiology is mandatory, but there are still many of us who ignore both signs and symptoms. The recent death of a colleague illustrates this. She complained of anal bleeding over a period of months but refused to consult her doctor because she was convinced that homoeopathy was the answer for the condition. When she was finally persuaded to have the bowel investigated, the cancer had spread to many of the surrounding organs and nothing could be done.

Irreparable harm can be done by the lay healer if they suggest that the patient ignores the advice of the doctor or stops his medication. The healer is not usually in the position to judge the reason for the advice given. For example, an inflamed appendix, if ignored or misdiagnosed may lead to peritonitis; a diabetic wrongly advised as to diet may become rapidly worse and may go into coma; and a badly manipulated back may lead to permanent injury.

'Be ye wise as serpents and harmless as doves', says St. Matthew. So we should err on the side of doing less rather than doing more, knowing that the correct amount and level of energy that the patient needs will flow through our hands without any extra interference from us, knowing also that to ask for help or advice brings no shame.

Every man is worth his hire and we should not be expected to work for no reward. We too need to live, we have bills to pay, families to feed.

What then should a healer charge?

The old saying 'not too little, not too much, but just enough' is valid advice here. To heal for nothing or for very little is inadvisable. Many of the people we meet who are in need, we will heal without charge: the very old, the very sick, close friends, our family. But if a patient other than these is able to pay for our time and our skill, a charge should be made. A doctor for example who does not charge is often thought less skilled than one who charges heavily. To get something for nothing suggests that the something is of little value. So make a charge for your services. Base this on the time spent in healing, the type of healing practised and the overhead costs, heating, lighting and other outgoings such as insurance. Don't be greedy!

Insurance. Again a factor to take into account in these days of litigation. Most insurance companies have a policy for the healer-practitioner.

It is important not only to be tidy and clean, but methodical. When your patient arrives, take down their name, address, date of birth, and telephone number. Keep a special file for this. Then let them talk, let them relax. Ask how you can help, ask about their symptoms, about family, fears, attitudes to life. Much healing is accomplished during this time. It is unlikely that they will tell you very much on their first visit, but it is important for you to know why they have come. Very often people tend to try you out, find out if you are any good, the information may tumble out almost incoherently, interspersed with what the wife thinks and irrelevant little opinions from all and sundry, including his own doctor who is frequently quoted as saying, 'Mr So-and-so I've never seen anything like this in my life'. Patients have frequently 'just missed [cancer, tuberculosis, pneumonia]', which is about as sensible as 'a touch of pregnancy'.

Keep notes: on progress, on what you see and feel, on future appointments, on everything. This is the way to learn. Use an appointment book and diary. Earnings may be taxed. Keep a record of payments.

It is not always necessary to see someone a second time

and often better to leave the question of a second visit to them, to their own judgement. If they feel that the treatment has helped they will certainly return. It will be clear after two or three appointments if your patient is improving. If not, ask a colleague if he or she would be willing to give treatment. There is no shame in this and no reflection on your own abilities.

Whole, holistic and holy; a healing is a relaxed and loving relationship between healer and patient. Whilst perhaps it is not possible yet for us to love everyone, we can like or at least feel compassion for the patient. We should never heal in a negative frame of mind or if we feel antagonism towards our patient.

To love, it is not necessary to enter emotionally into another's illness or his life circumstances. Try to avoid this and to be detached. Do not judge, for truth is only truth as the person sees it, and we can never be in possession of all the facts.

We are here to help people, to accept them as they are and not as we would like them to be. Try to see through the mass of emotion, of self-justification, of bitterness to the real needs within.

Remember that we ourselves are not the healer and it is by no merit of our own that the patient is helped. We are merely a means for the transmission of energies. Once we let that self-important person, the ego, get in the way, the healing will not come. The love will not flow.

Where should we do our healing? Well of course one can heal anywhere, in a bus, in the street but for preference we should have a warm quiet room. Soft music is helpful and it puts people at ease. Lighting and colours should not be too bright. If possible there should be no interruptions.

It is up to us to instil confidence and trust. We should tell our patient what we are about to do. Let her see us doing the healing with a quiet confidence, without recourse to notes or books, without hurry to finish. When all is ended, wash your hands to remove any static energy and remanence.

Sometimes when learning to heal you may feel tired and depleted. The patient may be drawing on your own energy. Alternatively, you may be wasting energy by unnecessary stress within yourself. This is good for neither of you. So relax for a few minutes, have a break, some fresh air, a few deep breaths. When you have been practising healing for a longer period of time you will find that the energy flow increases and that this particular problem is no more.

Never heal if you are tired or worried or out of sorts yourself; or if you feel disorientated in any way. At these times instead of giving energy the hands pick up the energies of the person that you are treating.

Trust the healing power. Don't doubt it. Don't worry if something out of the ordinary happens – a sudden pain, or your patient goes to sleep, or perhaps feels worse before feeling better. Don't be afraid if you seem to pick up the patient's symptoms. They will disappear.

What more can I tell you? We are all so different. Oh yes! Enjoy yourself – remember that you are contacting the Divine. A partnership with God is not to be sneezed at!

5
The Celestial Drainpipe

No two people are identical; it is understandable therefore that the amount of healing one person may receive is not the same amount as for another.

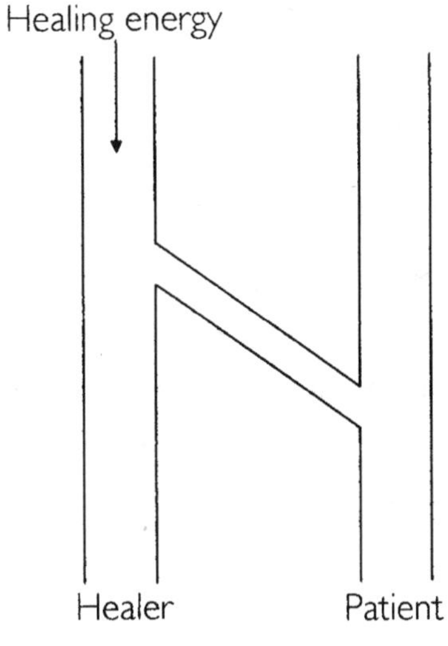

Celestial Drainpipe

Similarly no two healers are alike and the amount of healing transmitted by any one healer differs from that given by another. I used to wonder why this was so, since each healer draws on the same energies; and yet from one healer the amount received is not the same for every patient, and from a number of healers one single person seems to receive different amounts of energy.

Gradually a picture emerged. It was of a drainpipe, or rather two drainpipes side by side with a connecting link.

Energy passes through the healer to the patient. Many drainpipes are partially or completely blocked. Considering first the healer: one of the biggest blocks within the healer is pride. Whilst this is not usually evident in the beginning, after some success in giving healing, we tend to feel that we are the answer to the patient's prayer. 'Here I am, the healer. I have only to lay my hands upon you and you will be better.' And so he is, at first, but later strangely enough when we have forgotten that the energy is cosmic and God-given, the numbers benefiting from healing are fewer and fewer. This has happened to many many healers.

Greed is another block. Instead of seeing a sufferer entering the room one tends to see a cheque, or better still bank notes. 'Now, let me see, six times £25. That is £150 to pay in to the bank tomorrow.' After a time the patients stop coming because they do not feel any better.

Sloth: 'Well I'll give her a quick once over with my hands and she'll be satisfied.'

No she won't, and she leaves to find another healer who cares about her enough to do the job properly. And so we can go through all the deadly sins, each one leaving a nasty sludge within one's drainpipe until the pipe is blocked and practically nothing will flow through it.

So much for the healer, On the patient's side, the patient does not believe in healing, particularly healing by you. He has been pushed into it by the family or perhaps a friend. He does not really want to come and is not prepared to co-operate. Or he or she does not wish to be well; there are many advantages in being ill. Or your patient may want immediate results. Frequently we find that he is not ready to give up his life style (smoking, drugs, alcohol) and perhaps, after initial improvement, he falls back into the old ways.

Sometimes people try to get something for nothing. They plead poverty or demand reductions. But nothing is for nothing. One has to give, to get. Although it may not be money, it may be in kind. I have often been delighted to accept chocolate, scones, an original work of art (the patient's), or help in lieu of money. Sometimes too when the healing has gone as far as it can, your patient will become over dependent, enjoying the pleasant hour of chat, of warmth, of relaxation and the cup of tea. This also may be a block to further progress, which is strange, because it may be what she needs more than anything, but it draws too heavily upon the healer and no further energy can be given.

There are so many imponderables, but if the healer maintains purity of intent and the flow of love, healing will occur. All that we need is to keep faith with God and to have courage and love for others.

6
To Give A Healing

Giving healing to another is an act of love. It does not matter whether your patient is loveable or unloveable, when the healing flows, love flows also. For the energy that comes through and out of your hands is cosmic and comes from an area of absolute love.

Healing is a holy act, relating to the word holistic and given to the whole, to body, mind and spirit, with reverence.

It should therefore be done quietly for it has much to do with prayer. Never offer healing in a crowded noisy atmosphere; the amount of healing which will reach your patient will be minimal. But a quiet room, warm and comfortable, some pleasant music and perhaps flowers is ideal for what you wish to do.

It is important that your patient asks you for healing and that you do not force your (admirable) attentions upon them. Allow them to ask for healing because in doing this they will complete the link between healer and patient. So many eager healers feel that they are the answer to every situation, informing their victims that they are in need of healing and suggesting that they are ready and willing to perform this miraculous act. This is utterly wrong – the patient must request healing first and by this contribute to the whole. It is a little like refuelling a plane in mid-air. The tanker plane has the fuel but the connection must be made by the receiver plane or the fuel will be wasted.

Let us assume that you are both ready, your patient sitting on a stool, some gentle soft music, and you, the healer, standing behind. Put your hands gently on the shoulders for a little time. With your patient's welfare in your heart, ask within to be an instrument of healing. It does not matter how you ask. My own way of doing this is to ask God to put us both in the Light. The healing begins to flow through the palms of the hands.

The first stage in healing is in the fields around the body. Bring the palms of both hands to about twelve to nine inches from the body and move them gently inwards. A slight resistance may be felt as they touch the auric fields. Continue this repeatedly moving up and down the body, side to side, back to front. Allow the energies from your palms to flow inwards to the body.

Next we 'comb' the etheric body, uniting the earth energies at the base of the spine with the cosmic energy above the head. Standing behind, start at the bottom. One develops ways of doing this to suit oneself. My own method is to think of the basal energy in terms of a pool of liquid into which I dip my hands. Carrying the precious fluid in my palms close up the side of the body, over the outline of the shoulders and head, I pour it from one hand into the other when I reach the crown. Holding the second hand steady so as not to spill the energy, I reach up and draw down the cosmic energies from about eighteen inches above the head and unite the two, spreading the resultant energy over the body.

The next steps are best shown in the diagram which follows:

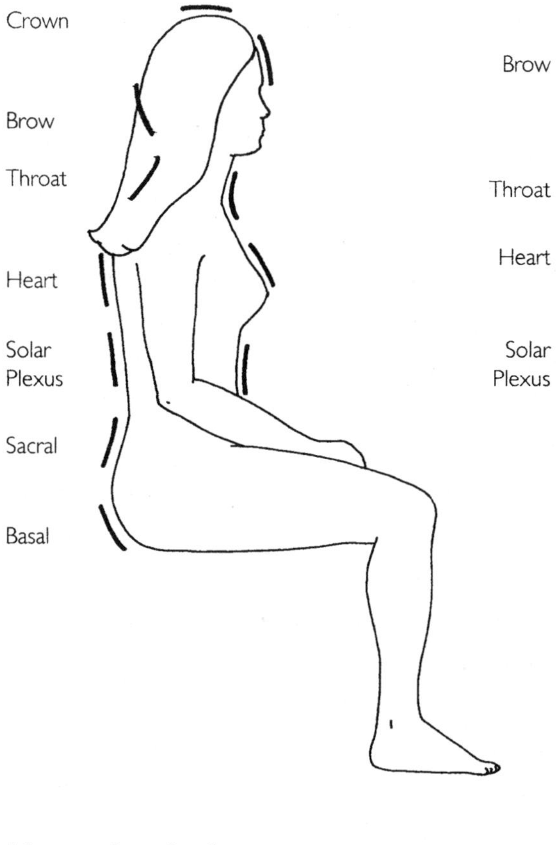

How to give a healing.
Diagram showing the chakras

Kneeling on the right of your patient, place the right hand on the solar plexus chakra in the front of the body and the left hand on the basal chakra behind. Allow the energy to flow from the one to the other (about 30-60 seconds). Then, keeping the hand on the solar plexus, move the left hand upwards to the sacral chakra. Again allow the energies to equalize. Move the left hand next to the solar plexus chakra at the back. Equalise the energies and then move the left hand to the heart chakra at the back in a similar way.

And so on up the body. Be careful at the throat centre and hold the front hand well away from the throat. In this way your patient won't feel that he is being strangled. Be particularly careful not to put hands on the lower chakras at the front. Again, your patient might feel threatened.

At the level of the brow chakra, draw both hands from front to back to encircle the head. This clears the lower aspects of the third eye which allows one to have complete awareness from every direction.

Your mother perhaps said, 'I have eyes in the back of my head!' How right she was!

Lastly, end the healing with a gentle touch or kiss on the head and return the hands to the shoulders.

7
The Practice of Meditation

MEDITATION IS something that we can do for ourselves, a special kind of relaxed awareness. It brings in relaxation and exercises some sort of control over areas where we have least control, over our thoughts. It aids the development of our spiritual growth and decreases stress and tension. From the peaceful centre of our being we can then think and act in a balanced manner.

Because our awareness is heightened and our own centre is quiet we are able to listen outwardly to other people and can also listen inwardly. We realize that subtle changes are taking place within ourselves and this brings an understanding of how our physical and emotional states can be affected by our feelings.

When the mind is silent and we have trained it to focus and listen, other understandings and insights may enter. We are no longer blocking the free passage of healing or inspired knowledge.

So how do we meditate? There are many meditation

techniques, culled from many parts of the world and it is advisable to choose one of them and stick to it.

But before doing that there are certain basic suggestions:

If possible meditation should be done in a firm upright chair or sitting crosslegged on the floor, holding the back erect but not tense. It is important not to slump.

Organise the least possible number of interruptions. Do such things as disconnecting the phone. If necessary, lock the door. Choose a time when you are likely to be alone.

Practise for at least ten minutes daily even though it may not at first seem to be working.

Don't meditate for too long. Ten minutes once or twice daily will do more than hours of forced attention (which is not meditation).

Inner and Outer Focus Meditation

Perhaps the two simplest types of meditation are those concerned with awareness of breathing.

The first is an inner focus exercise.Sit comfortably, shut your eyes and be aware of your breathing. Feel the breath coming in, going out. Feel your chest and abdomen moving as you breathe. Pay attention to the breath, ignoring any sounds or thoughts, any bodily sensations or feelings. Give the breath complete undivided attention for at least five minutes.

The outer focus meditation uses some object outside the self, e.g. a candle, and combines this with the inner breath exercise but keeping the eyes open.

The two types of exercise produce slightly different brainwave patterns. The first blocks out sensory experience. Both exercises are about self control and tend to focus within ourselves, separate from the world. Having the eyes shut reduces the number of distractions.

The outer focus meditation gives a special meditative awareness and a readiness to respond to situations without an emotional reaction. Open-eyed exercises affect our brain waves in such a way that a kind of mental centredness is enhanced. This helps us to be more focused and less influenced by our environment.

A variation of inner and outer focus meditations may be as follows:

Inner focus. Sit relaxed as before. Think of an easily visualised symbol, a cross or a circle, a form with a well-defined centre. Use the same design for every meditation. Visualise this during the whole time.

Outer focus. Sit, relax. Rest your hand in front of you, so that you can see the thumbnail with eyes lowered. Look intently at it but do not strain your eyes. Keep the eyes and eyelids relaxed. Be aware of the movement of your breath and watch the thumbnail attentively.

Both the above types of meditation can be done anywhere without attracting any attention.

Passive or active exercises

The passive exercises involve observing our thoughts without doing anything with them. The unconscious sends up a thought about once a minute. We must be aware of them without becoming involved with them. We ask the mind-talk to be still whilst we are doing this. If both are still we may attain a true deep silence in the mind. In the active exercise, we ask the subconscious to be still and not to send up thoughts, and we give the perpetual talker something to do, something very boring so that it falls silent after a time. Depending on one's own personality the introvert will find the passive exercise easier; the extrovert will prefer the active way.

Passive exercise. Sit relaxed. Tell yourself that you are going to relax mentally. Let your mind drift, thinking about nothing in particular. Allow thoughts to form and fade again without trying to control or analyse them. Just let them come and go in obscurity.

Active exercise. Sit relaxed. Count breaths up to ten and repeat again and again throughout the practise time. When you lose count start again. Believe me, it's boring!

Exercises which concentrate our attention on the breath or other physical processes help us to be more centred and earthed. But if your body is uncomfortable or if there are physical problems, a mental focus might be better.

Mental exercise. Sit relaxed. Choose one of the higher colours, e.g. blue, and visualize it as a sphere.

Sensory exercise. Sit, relax, become aware of the breath. Notice exhalation and then be aware of the shift where the breath changes and keep your mind focused on that.

And so on.

There are as many techniques of meditation as there are peas in a pod and these are but a few of them. Choose one for yourself. There is no wrong technique, only the best for the moment. Start with something simple and stick with it for several weeks. If your mind seems to wander off, bring it back and continue. Don't give up!

8
Contacting The Sixth Sense

The Art of Dowsing

THE ANCIENT science of channelling the natural energies of the earth has long been ignored in the West although it is still practised in the East. In China it is known as Feng Shui. There, it is still recognised that the shape and form of the land is important to the welfare of those who live on its surface and that the negative flow of energies within the earth can be altered and adapted to the benefit of man.

The great German physician, Hahnemann (1755 – 1843), who pioneered the science of homoeopathy, postulated that there were certain patterns of disease affecting the human body. He called them *miasms*.

Originating in the subtle fields surrounding the body, these patterns spread their influence throughout all the energies of our being. They are essentially a disharmony of energies within us. Miasms are acquired by various contagious or traumatic influences that we come into contact with during our lives. They show their effect through the body systems; electrical, physiological, and biochemical. Depending on the intensity of the vibration, the pattern may become encoded genetically or by resonance, that is to say it may come through the parents or may be acquired during your lifetime when the cause may be a bacterial or viral attack or come from toxic pollution in the food or in the environment. The disease focus itself may be an area of weakness in a particular part of the body, the site being genetically determined or following a traumatic event or exposure to disharmonious energy. There are many examples of cancer, for instance, with a previous history of injury at the site where the malignancy develops at a later date, or the development of malignant tumours in areas which have been exposed to carcinogenic agents such as the oil used in spinning, where we find the later development of Mule-spinners cancer (carcinoma of the scrotum). Farmers, breathing in fungal spores from mouldy hay, frequently develop Farmers Lung; smokers, lung and throat cancers and heart disease. The disease tendency may lie dormant for years, not manifesting fully until the tissues are weakened by external or internal causes. It may however show in minor ways, in minor bodily stress patterns such as headaches, aching joints, and gastrointestinal upsets.

When the distortion of the energy pattern becomes gross, more severe bodily dysfunction may be seen with biological dysfunction and loss of vitality. This is disease as we know it, often reversible, but also often incurable.

Incurable? Yet it should be possible to rearrange the energy patterns in such a way that they are once again in harmony. And we know that this can be done through healing, more so in the early stages of the disease but from time to time we have what is generally considered a 'miracle cure'. We tend to think of miracle cures as the province of the healer, the acupuncturist, and those outside the practice of conventional medicine, but this is not so. There was no greater miracle cure than the first treatment of penicillin, or the treatment of diabetes with insulin, of pernicious anaemia with Vitamen B12; all previously incurable conditions.

In surgery also, the removal and replacement of a diseased part, the replacement, for example, of a kidney has given future life to those who would otherwise have died. These are all miracles, brought about through skill, research and understanding of the human condition. The miracle of life has always been beyond our comprehension but whilst life persists, man will ever try to explain it.

This book is concerned with methods of healing other than conventional medicine and surgery but let us not be too highhanded and superior in our way of thinking, disregarding the tremendous benefits of conventional medicine without which many of us would not be here to read these pages.

When you are a healer, a doctor or a lay healer, and when you care beyond anything else about the well being of others, a sixth sense seems to come into being: Sight, Hearing, Touch, Taste and Smell, and now Knowing. Perhaps we should call it Understanding. Whatever we call it, it is there, and yet we still doubt its power. How then can we prove to ourselves that this sixth sense exists?

The answer is by *dowsing*. Dowsing is an ancient and much tried method of finding out, not just about people or illness but about anything under the sun; information which is not known to the conscious mind but can be known to the subconscious.

Dowsing seems to transcend normal concepts of space and time so that it is possible to find out both the future and the past. One can date archaeological sites, find out how long things have laid in the ground, find the age of trees without counting the rings, and in matters of space find a missing person from a map or perhaps find one's way home without a compass. It gives a strange ability to the dowser. It doesn't fit at all well into the orthodox way of doing things, doesn't follow any accepted norms.

Dowsing opens up a natural sensitivity which allows us to know things which we cannot know by the use of our physical senses or by our thinking brain. It has been shown by many investigators that it is a function of the right brain. The brain patterns alter; the normal beta frequencies, which are the active state, change and the brain waves become slower. Our normal state of consciousness changes.

Many different techniques are used by dowsers. Most of them are based on the use of rods or a pendulum, which in itself has no virtue, but is simply an extension of the consciousness of the dowser. Almost anything can be used as a pendulum. The material has very little importance, for it is only an instrument which makes our own faculties more easily visible. There are however, certain obvious limitations: a light pendulum outdoors is useless as it tends to be blown by the wind, and dowsing rods are cumbersome indoors.

To dowse we must have a neutral state of mind. We should not have any preconceived ideas about the answer. If we do, we will find that the rods or the pendulum will turn the way we anticipate and the whole exercise is nullified. People will say, as their pendulum swings the way that they wish it to swing, 'I thought that was the answer.' This is the answer that is probably the wrong one.Dowsing should be done in a detached frame of mind, unconcerned about the outcome, about what the answer will be. At the beginning this is extremely hard to do. Sometimes the answer is the exact opposite of what we anticipated, sometimes it is very difficult to reach. Sometimes we are too emotionally involved in a question. When that happens, it is better to ask someone else to do the investigation.

There is only one way to find out about dowsing and that is by personal experience. Try, and if it seems to go wrong, try again. In the next chapter we will discuss the way to do this and give a little more detail of the pitfalls awaiting us.

9
Practical Dowsing

In the last chapter we hinted at the hidden knowledge that is available to us when we begin to dowse and it might be interesting to expand on this a little.

As might be expected, the finding of water heads the list. The location of underground water is vital in many countries of the world, but the finding of underground streams will also affect siting of buildings and the building of major waterways. The dowser, having found water, needs to know the purity, the quantity and the depth of the stream and whether the water is static or running. All this is done before the ground is opened.

The same is true when looking for oil or gas, for minerals or precious stones.

On building sites the location of cables and fractured pipes is often necessary.

We mentioned archaeological sites; here also the depth is important and the dates of anything found by digging. Finding the initial site is often done through the technique of map dowsing. Sunken ships and buried treasure are occasionally found in this way.

Dowsers are often asked to locate missing persons. Some dowsers are employed by the police. In a recent murder case a dowser was asked by the police to try to find the body of the victim. The murder was in the west of England but the dowser pinpointed a grave in a wood in Kent. On opening the grave a body was found, the body of a woman. This was not the body of the original murder victim who still remains to be found. Even the most reliable dowsers can make mistakes.

Medical diagnosis and the selection of remedies, homoeopathic or otherwise, is an area where dowsing can be a very valuable help, and so also is the detection of adverse energies in the home; a fascinating side of healing which we will deal with in a later chapter.

A dowser should ideally stick to the area in which he or she is interested. You will find that not all these aspects of dowsing will appeal to you. We don't all want to find buried bodies and rarely have an opportunity to look for treasure ships, we are not universally good in every field. But if we are interested and if we practise we can get reliable results in the areas of our choice. So let us begin.

How to Use a Pendulum

A pendulum is a weight which is suspended on a thread or chain of about six to ten inches in length, and can be made of brass or some similar substance. I have several pendulums. I find that the brass ones which are heavier are best if I use them outside but for inside work I use a quartz or plastic pendulum.

The next step is to establish the difference between a yes and a no. To do this we must ask a question where we can verify the answer. For example, we can hold the pendulum over a part of our body, say a leg, and ask 'Is this my left side?', or 'Is this my right side?' In this way we can establish the yes or the no, and so on. Not really very hard.

This is an easy example, but as we progress we find that the hardest part of dowsing is not to allow the critical part of the brain, the left brain, to take charge of the situation. It is important that we are neither positive or negative in our thinking, that we remain neutral in our expectations. If we care too much about an outcome, then let someone else do the dowsing.

We should ask the right question and make the question specific using the logical side of our brain (the left brain), and then allow the right brain to give us the answer. There must be a need to know.

You could begin in the following way:

1. Rest your elbow on a table, holding the chain at the top. Let it swing idly.
2. Keeping the hand still, will the pendulum to swing to and fro. When it is doing this, tell the pendulum to swing in another direction, say, side to side.
3. Take a circular protractor. Hold the pendulum over the centre of the protractor with the zero on the protractor furthest away. Go through the same drill of telling the pendulum to swing in various directions. Make it follow the meridians of the protractor. Now make it circle clockwise and anticlockwise.
4. When the pendulum is doing what you tell it to do, you are ready to use it; not before.

The next thing to do is to decide on the type of question that you are going to ask and on the meaning of the response.

The question must be unambiguous, one which has either a positive or a negative answer. Suppose you want to test hen's eggs to see if they are fertilized. A simple question is enough. 'Is this egg fertilized?' But if we want to know if it will rain, to say, 'Will it rain today?' is an ambiguous question. It will rain. It is bound to rain somewhere. So we must be very clear what questions we ask. Beware of the question with more than one answer.

Various methods can be used to find the positive or negative reply of the pendulum. Hold it by the right hand over the right side of the body and ask for the positive or 'yes'. Usually this is a clockwise swing but it is occasionally anticlockwise, so it should be asked on each occasion. Alternatively ask a question where the answer is known, such as 'Am I a woman/man?'

Anticlockwise is usually 'No'. A swing forwards and backwards indicates, 'Rephrase the question' or 'Don't know'.

Try the following three exercises.

1. Take six small envelopes containing either (1) sugar, (2) salt or (3) coffee, and mark them A, B, C, D, E, and F. Place them in a row on the table in front of you. Select one of them and using the pendulum ask the following question. 'Is the content of this envelope ...[sugar],[salt],[coffee]...?' This means that the question must be asked for three times for each envelope. Chart the results.

	1	2	3	4	5	6
sugar						
salt						
coffee						

Now take one packet which has not yet been opened and ask, 'Will I like the contents?' The pendulum should give an equivocal answer, swinging to and fro.

2. The next exercise deals with polarity: finding the pendulum movements specific to yourself. Individual polarity is a subject of great importance. It will show you why the pendulum will move for you in the way it does.

The human body may be polarised either positively or negatively, and the pendulum reactions are affected by this polarity.

Obtain a simple bar magnet and place it on the table in front of you. Take a non-magnetic pendulum and hold it over the north end of the magnet, the positive end, and note the result. Repeat this over the south end of the magnet, the negative end, and again note the result.

If the pendulum gyrates clockwise or oscillates to the right when placed over the north end and gyrates anticlockwise or oscillates to the left over the south end you are said to have normal polarity. Your future pendulum answers will probably be:

Clockwise – positive – yes

Anti-clockwise – negative – no

We now have two types of answers, detection of answers to questions and detection of polarity.

3. The pendulum can be used to obtain a third type of answer: the detection of boundaries to energy fields.

For example, we can detect the radiation around a TV set. Try this with the television switched on, and then off. Note any difference in the extent of the fields.

Think of the pendulum as an extension of your own body, complete with nerves, so that its message or messages can be received by your own consciousness. Try to cultivate a disinterested outlook. Merely record the message consciously. For if you use your pendulum with the intense desire to find or gain data you may create the data desired and run into error. Don't let your own concepts and beliefs interfere with what you are looking for. And don't worry.

It takes time and application to become a good dowser. We all make mistakes in the beginning.

10
Disease and Adverse Energies

All the world vibrates. You, me, the world itself. There is absolutely nothing which does not vibrate. Even apparently dead rocks; even 'dead' tissues have their own rates of vibration as they break down to form simpler compounds. From the sounds that we hear to the tissues that we see, from the cells of the little finger to the complex mechanisms of the brain; from the grass beneath our feet to the molecules of oxygen in the air; vibrating fields of energy, each field vibrating at its own rate and at its own natural frequency.

Very few people can see these subtle fields of energy but their effects can be seen. If they were not there, we would not be here either. The building blocks of matter, atoms, are also composed of energy fields. Within an atom the electrons are held in orbit moving as planets move around our Sun, each in its own orbit mathematically spaced from each other. The closer to the centre, the higher the energy of the electron; and the gross result is matter, something which we can all see and with which we are familiar. Atoms can be stable or unstable, depending on their electrical charge and the number of electrons in their orbits. The unstable ones form compounds readily, the stable ones retain their individuality. Alter the temperature or the pressure and the rate of vibration is altered. If we think of a substance such as water, at nought degrees centigrade the normally fluid water solidifies and becomes ice. The rate of vibration of the molecules is lower. At one hundred degrees centigrade the molecular vibration alters again. Energy is released and the new form is a gas, steam.

Electric and magnetic fields are the observable results of the interaction of energies in the subtle state. They are like interference patterns between two or more fields of energy. Normally the energy fields are balanced harmoniously, not only within their own system but with surrounding fields of energy. The direction of energies is naturally towards harmony or towards a balanced state. The positive and negative charges of the individual components make for either a harmonious or disharmonious pattern. So harmony or balance at one point has direct bearing on another. The same is true of disharmony, which, like harmony, can spread from one system to another.

If one energy field can affect another field, is it possible to alter the second field? We know that this can happen. We know, for instance, that high frequency cosmic rays can disturb atomic structure to the degree that new elements are formed. We know also that irradiation can change the vibrating frequencies within matter. Irradiation of some semi-precious stones can change their colour so that they resemble true precious stones of much greater value and can be sold as such. The rate of frequency of the vibrating molecules within the stone is altered and with it the colour. Irradiation of animal tissues by certain radioactive elements can produce changes within the tissue. This is the basis for irradiation of cancerous tumours. However the changes are not always beneficial. In the early days of X-ray treatment it was not unusual for the technicians to lose fingers or to lose potency. Clockmaking firms employed workers to paint the hands of watches with luminous paint so that the hands could be seen in the dark. The radioactive paint had disastrous effects on the workers and the practice was ended. Mistakes in over-irradiation still occur with horrid consequences.

When I first qualified at the end of the second world war, an epidemic of ringworm of the scalp was raging. The accepted treatment was depilation of the scalp by X-rays; that is, a dose of X-rays was given to cause the existing hairs to fall. When the new hair regrew it was clear of fungus. One day, shortly after a public holiday, two little boys with scalp ringworm were given doses of X-rays. The machine was so adapted that an overdose could not be given, but in the holiday period someone had tampered with it and altered the setting. The children received a massive overdose. True their hair fell out, but then the skin broke down and the skull bones disintegrated leaving the brain exposed and this in turn disintegrated also. It was my job at the time to dress the resultant wounds daily until, mercifully for them, the little boys died.

Skin and tissues can accept only a small dose of X-rays before they break down. Above that dose, irreversible changes take place and the molecular structure of the tissues is altered. In practice the number of units given is carefully monitored so that not more than 1500 roentgen units is given to any one area in a lifetime as the treatment has a summation effect. Small doses given repeatedly over a long period can add up to the larger dose required for treatment. The total amount varies according to the tissue.

So one field of activity in the energy sense can affect another and taking this one stage further, it is possible that the patterns of vibration of subatomic energy might be affected by the energies of thought or emotion. We have no proof of this, nothing that could stand up to scientific investigation but there is a possibility that a person who is in harmony in these areas might affect his subatomic physical state, or the subatomic state of others. Have you ever noticed that happy people are rarely ill and that happiness spreads to those around them and into their surroundings? One can feel happiness and peace and calm on entering the room. Conversely, a disharmonious person has the opposite effect. Around an angry or depressed person all seems to go wrong. They seem to impregnate everything they touch with the inharmonious energy. Never eat food cooked by an angry cook or if you do so, have the indigestion pills handy!

In human relationships we modify each other all the time. The stronger personality influences the weaker, the one resonating with and changing the natural frequencies of the other, whether it be thought, emotion or denser tissues.

In 1952 Professor Harold Burr published his book, *Blueprint for Immortality*. In it he postulated that changes in electrical potential are in the nature of a controlling field; a blueprint upon which the body is built, and that changes in the fields of energy surrounding the body can imprint themselves upon the controlling field and, depending upon the way that the controlling field is modified, can produce change within the human body tissues of either regeneration or degeneration.

Man is a very complex bioelectric and biomagnetic being. The nervous system resembles a computer in that it is a complex of fields and forces, of electrical currents and charges, with information-gathering, -storage and -retrieval facilities, far in advance of the most advanced computer made by man. It emits electromagnetic energies, mostly at lower frequencies which are in particular concerned with brain waves and heart function. It is this radiation which is probably the organising field in the body and which is influenced by the controlling field or blueprint.

We live in an environment in which natural electrical and magnetic energies play a considerable role. The Earth itself generates a weak geomagnetic field of about fifty microtessa in which all living systems have evolved and within which they are able to exist in a balanced state. But during the last two centuries and in particular in the last fifty years the strength of the field has been artificially increased and it is now having a profound effect on the magnetic field of the Earth. Man's contribution to the environment in the way of electromagnetic radiation comes from radar and communications systems, from radio and television transmission, from power lines, microwave ovens and many household electrical appliances. People who are exposed to electromagnetic fields by way of their jobs, particularly if the field is higher than normal, tend to develop a range of diseases, particularly cancer. In 1977 the USA Embassy in Moscow was found to have been irradiated from 1953 to 1976 with a field of low intensity. Three US ambassadors serving there during that period died of cancer.

The geomagnetic field of the Earth varies, and contains vertical oscillating waves of a fundamental basic frequency. The waves run in a natural frequency which is repeated many times in a second. The harmonics extend into the megahertz range; these are called Schumann waves and are naturally occurring. For their conductivity they seem to need a reasonable level of moisture in the soil. Once the water level has dropped, as, for example, in a period of drought or around a large town their conductivity is reduced. In addition the waves are said to be unable to pass through concrete and particularly through reinforced concrete. The Schumann wave is beneficial to man. The absence of the waves can be tolerated for some time by healthy people but people who are already sick are in need of their effect.

One wonders whether an understanding of this lies behind the old custom of sending invalids for convalescence to the country or to the seaside.

Geopathic Stress

The earth's energy field is inconstant. In some places there is background radioactivity from rocks and soil. In this country this is particularly so in areas of Cornwall. Of the other energies some are more harmful than others. Of those known, two form a network covering the surface of the earth which is also covered with ley lines of positive energy. The two networks are called the Curry Grid and the Hartman Net.

The *Curry Grid* was found by Dr Manfred Curry who had a research clinic in Southern Germany. Like so many of the major discoveries it was recorded almost by accident. Dr Curry had been investigating the reaction distance of the human energy field; that is to say the point at which the energy field could be recorded. He found that one group of patients had a reaction distance of 0 – 40 cm and another group a distance of 60 – 100 cm. Cancer patients had usually

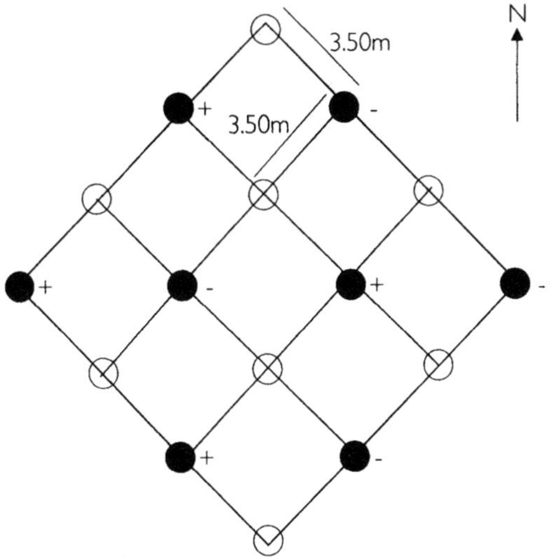

The Curry Grid

a reaction distance greater than the former two groups and of more than 140 cm. It was during these investigations that he observed an energy network which we now call the Curry Grid. The network was of terrestial origin and consisted of alternate bands of energy, 3.5 to 4.0 metres apart and running diagonally from south to west and north to east. It seemed to be stable and the bands had a width of about 80 cm. The bands or lines were charged alternately positive and negative. Where the grid lines intersected with lines of similar charges, there was marked geopathic disturbance.

Curry also noted that the + + crossings lengthened the

reaction distance and the - - crossings shortened it. As a result of his studies he concluded that the crossing points of both types were harmful to man if he were exposed to them for a long period of time.

The *Hartmann Net* or *Global Grid* is thought to be of cosmic origin. It has a smaller grid pattern running east – west and north – south. It seems to be more unstable than the Curry Grid and the bands of energy composing it change every six hours; at sunrise, noon, sunset and midnight. At these times it may disappear for a short period.

According to Dr Hartmann it only becomes harmful when there is a sharp change in the weather.

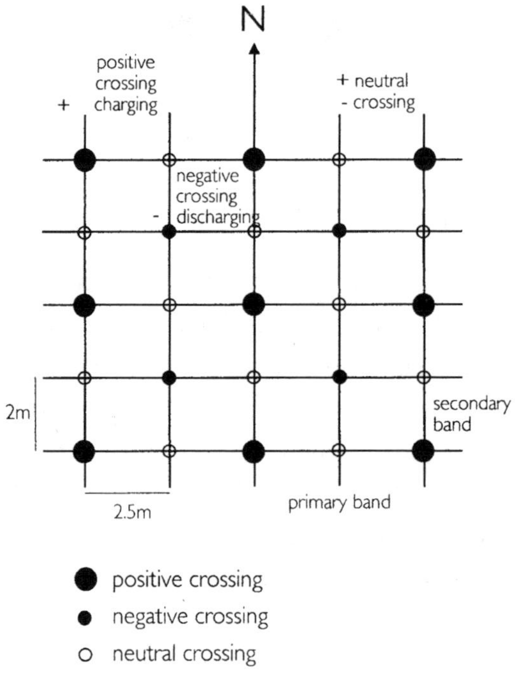

The Hartmann Grid

The third major factor in the production of geopathic stress is associated with underground water flowing under pressure or through hollows in the rocks. These underground streams can cause an increase in geomagnetic intensity which can influence living organisms. Where two streams cross, even though they may be running at different levels, the intensity of negative radiation may be harmful. Streams on the surface allowed to flow freely do not show the same negative intensity.

Almost all the research on zones of geopathic stress has been carried out in Germany, Austria and the USSR. The results have been startling.

The Institute of Hygiene at the University of Heidelberg and the Electrophysical Institute at Munich together investigated a house in the Neckar Valley where three generations had died of cancer. It was found that the sleeping bed was located over a geological fracture. Mice were placed in cages over the site of the bed and in a neutral area. Those over the geopathic disturbance were restless, bit each other and ate their young. In the neutral area of the control cage, the mice behaved normally.

In 1979 at a conference in Riga, Latvia, it was stated that there was an increase of disease in patients living over harmful radiations. The diseases cited included brain dysfunction and other mental disturbances, bronchial asthma and cancer. At the same conference, the doctor in charge of a large regional hospital showed that 20% of the seriously ill people suffering from a variety of diseases improved markedly when their beds were moved out of an area of geopathic stress.

Many doctors on the continent, in Vienna and in Berlin, are so convinced of the incidence and importance of geopathic stress as a cause of disease that they have advised all their patients with cancer to move their beds or have their home investigated by a dowser. Among them is Dr Hans Nieper from Hanover. In his book *Revolution in Technology, Medicine and Society* he states, 'according to studies I have initiated, at least 92% of all the cancer patients that I have examined have remained for long periods in geopathic zones.' This referred especially to the sleeping area. In 1985 while lecturing in America, he said, 'this does not necessarily say that geopathic zones or their magnetic effects produce cancer, but rather it is the ultimate push button that then makes the thing happen'. It has been suggested that the geopathic force is sufficiently strong to overcome the natural balance of the body's energy or to affect the energy field of the body adversely, making the patient more vulnerable to disease.

People who have been subjected to geopathic stress often show non-specific symptoms at the onset. Many people complain of sleep disturbances; restless legs or cramp in bed are symptomatic as are mood changes in the waking hours. All these symptoms do of course have many other causes and this is a factor which should always be borne in mind.

If it is thought that someone is suffering from geopathic stress, it is advisable to suggest that he changes his sleeping site, either by moving his bed or sleeping in another room. Often a small change of this sort is sufficient, particularly if the geopathic stress covers only a small localised area of the room. The body gradually corrects itself, sleep becomes normal and the symptoms disappear. If the symptoms continue then a more specialised approach may be necessary. Sometimes if a patient has slept over a geopathic zone for a long time, the symptoms become 'locked in', that is they tend to persist. These people would be advised to contact a healer who is also a dowser. Specialised measures may be needed to restore the balance of the patient's own energies and the zone of negative energy should be neutralised. An expert dowser should be capable of doing this.

Geopathic stress zones may not always be a factor in the development of disease but may affect behaviour in young children or young people or indeed any place where people are assembled for any length of time, such as a place of work. An illuminating book written by an Austrian teacher, Kaethe Bachler, illustrates this point. Kaethe Bachler after hearing about geopathic stress came to the idea that harmful earth radiation might play some part in the difficulties of mentally slow children. Many of her children gave a normal performance at school when their beds were resited. As a result of her observations she was given a research programme by the Pedagogical Institute in Salzburg. The aim was to establish the relationship, if any, between geopathic stress and school performance. The research was carried out in 1972, and her book *Discoveries of a Dowser* was published in 1978. Miss Bachler in the course of her research tested three thousand homes and interviewed eleven thousand people in fourteen countries. She proved that 95% of slow learners and other children with learning problems slept over either water crossings or Curry crossings or both. She also interviewed five hundred people suffering from both cancerous and benign growths and showed that in all cases the patient had been exposed to two geopathic factors at least; one or more underground water crossings, or water under a Curry line crossing.

An independent observation by a headmaster of a school

for children with learning difficulties noted that all their beds had been over geopathic zones. He plotted the radiation lines and found that in every case one went through the head area of the bed whilst in children who stuttered, the radiation crossed the area of the throat.

The development of electromagnetic energy for power and communications is widely considered to be one of the great achievements of modern man. Although it has led to technological progress, it is doubtful whether the energies involved are totally beneficial. There are few places left on earth which are free of man-made electromagnetic radiations.

In the 1960s Dr. Robert Becker, working in the USA, developed a hypothesis that healing and growth were controlled by tiny self-generated electrical signals which governed cellular activity. In 1973 he had begun to use tiny electric currents applied through implanted electrodes to cure broken human bones which would not knit properly. He was worried that this type of treatment could get out of hand and reasoned that if an electric current could influence benign growth it might also cause malignant growth. Because of his knowledge in these fields Becker was asked to undertake a study of extremely low frequency currents (ELF currents). The American navy at this time was developing an extensive antenna system in Northern Wisconsin for communication purposes. It was feared that this might have environmental and health hazards. The form of electrical energy emitted was also extremely low frequency non-ionizing electromagnetic radiation. From the results obtained in Becker's work, it became clear that the radiation could produce a lowering of bodily resistance.

It was during this period of investigation that Becker

became aware that ELF currents were similar to but weaker than high voltage power lines (765,000 volt lines). Attention was now centred on possible health risks from the electromagnetic fields of these overhead cables. Laboratory data showed that these fields were indeed a hazard and had a deleterious effect on animal growth particularly in the second generation. In the late 1970s Stephen Perry reported that he had begun to see numerous cases of clinical depression among people who lived near overhead power lines. A further survey showed an increase of suicides in areas affected by high levels of non-ionizing radiation.

In 1979, a report found that in several hundred homes close to high current power distribution lines, the death rate for cancer for children under nineteen was twice the expected rate. There was also a significant correlation between the presence of power lines and adult cancer. Similar connections were found between cancer and radiation emitted by microwave devices and radar.

In Britain, the awareness of possible health hazards from power lines and cables began in the mid 70s. The village of Fishpond in Dorset was the subject of an enquiry into the effect of overhead power lines on health. The village was crossed and recrossed with overhead electric cables. Villagers complained of a range of illnesses from migraine and sleeplessness to blackouts, heart disease and cancer. The enquiry confirmed the connection between the power fields and cancer, in particular childhood leukaemias.

This world is indeed a dangerous place, and man in his psychological and ecological expansion a very dangerous being. Many of the negative geomagnetic phenomena may be man-produced in the sense that stresses, strains and disharmonies are created at intersections and boundaries by mining and quarrying, by drilling for oil and water, lowering the water table, and even by the laying of sewage and drainage pipes. Many electric cables are also carried beneath the surface of the ground. We hope to show in a later chapter how we may in some way alter the negativity by blocking or diverting the flow of these negative energies.

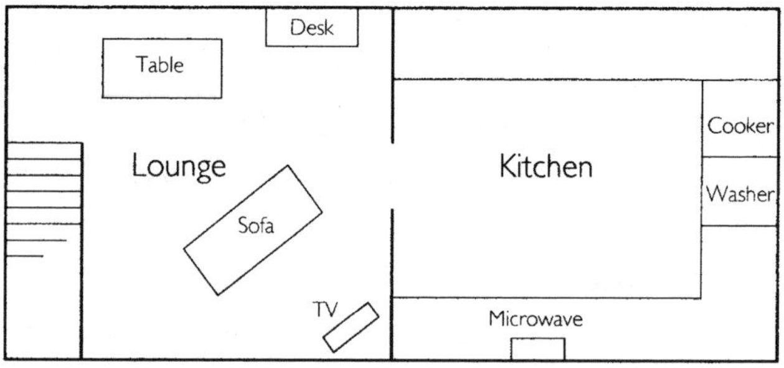

Ground floor plan

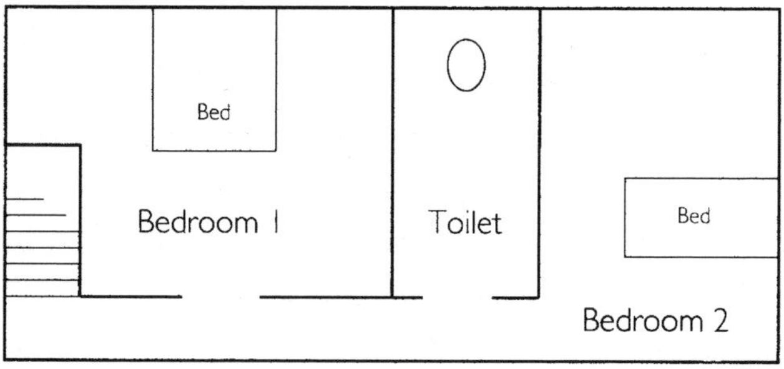

First floor plan

House plan

11
Map Dowsing

Once you are fairly confident in using your pendulum, try to use it to find negative energies.

Draw the ground plan of a house or building that you know. Preferably this should not be the house in which you live. The reason for this is that most of us have preconceived ideas about our own house.

Hold the pendulum over the plan and ask, 'Are there any adverse energies in this building?'

If the answer is 'yes', take your pendulum and moving slowly around the outside wall of the diagram, ask, 'Is there adverse energy here?' If there are negative energies entering or leaving at any point your pendulum will give a positive swing. Mark the point with a X. When the circuit of the plan is complete you may have several crosses marked. You then need to know the points of entry of the negative energy and the points of exit, so that you may block the point of entry. Frame your question accordingly. The plan will now

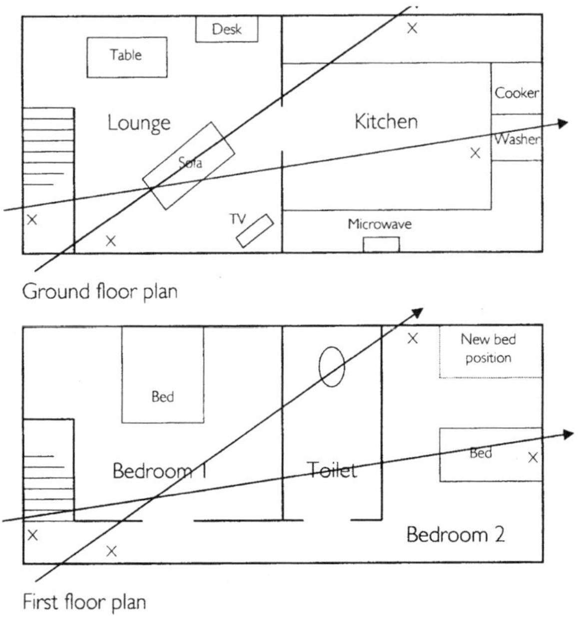

House plan with energy llines

look like the diagram above.

Join the crosses and arrow the direction of flow.

Note that in the plan, the lines cross beneath the sofa where the occupants of the house sit to watch T.V. Move the sofa quickly to an area where it is not under fire!

Now consider the upstairs floor. Perhaps they sleep in Bedroom 2. Horror! The negative energy line goes through the site of the bed. It's not as bad as the sofa where two lines cross but definitely not good. Move the bed.

Bedroom 1 seems all right. The toilet has minimal occupancy. Remind the people who live in the house not to sit there and read the paper!

Next. Think of other sources of negative energy which might be in the house and dowse for these.

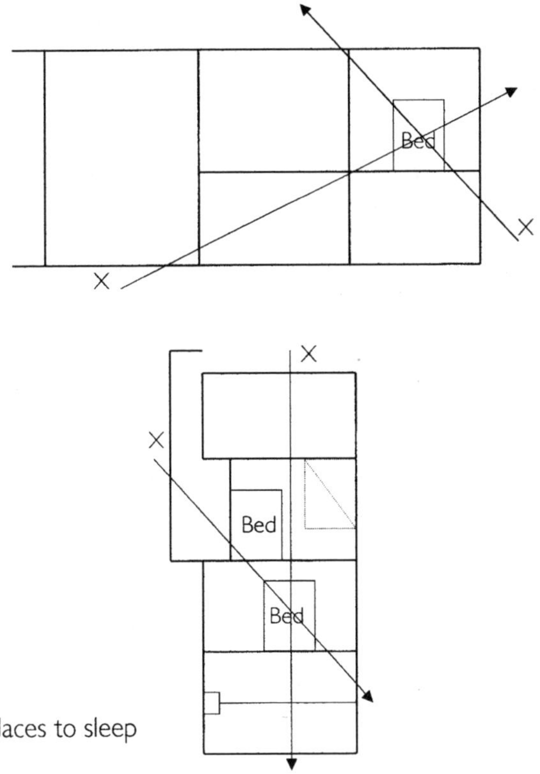

Dangerous places to sleep

1. Is the house a happy one (this means the people)? If not:
2. Is there anger, or unhappiness of any sort, going on?
3. What has happened in the house in the past? Past happenings, even recent happenings often leave their mark, and if the house is an old one, many people have lived, and died in it, often tragically.
4. Finally, and very rarely, is there a ghost or bad influence?

I put the last in because of a house which I was asked to dowse. The request came by post. I was sent the plan of a house in its own grounds and asked to offer advice as to adverse energies within the property. On dowsing I found that every stream of negative energy had been already blocked at the garden boundary. I suspected a trap but continued dowsing. There was a ley line running east – west just outside the garden. There were also two very strange features, one in the garden and one inside the house. The one in the garden was rounded and had a very positive energy. I wondered if it could have been the site of a small building. My answer was, No. Could it have some religious significance? Question phrased wrongly. Some sort of healing area? Yes. In the very distant past? No. I left it there.

The second area inside the house was moving. It was a small area confined to two rooms but it changed its position frequently. Feeling rather a fool, I said in my written report, 'Is it possible that you have a small ghost?' The reply came a few days later. It confirmed that all adverse energies leading into the property had been blocked. The area in the garden had originally been used for a circle sending out distant healing while the house was in the process of being altered. The letter ended, 'How clever of you to find our ghost. He is the man who originally built our house and he strongly disapproves of the use of our house for healing.'

I could tell you many stories of the houses that I have dowsed for people who have been ill or who have been unhappy, but it is better that you find your own. This is a very interesting aspect of dowsing and very rewarding. The results can be

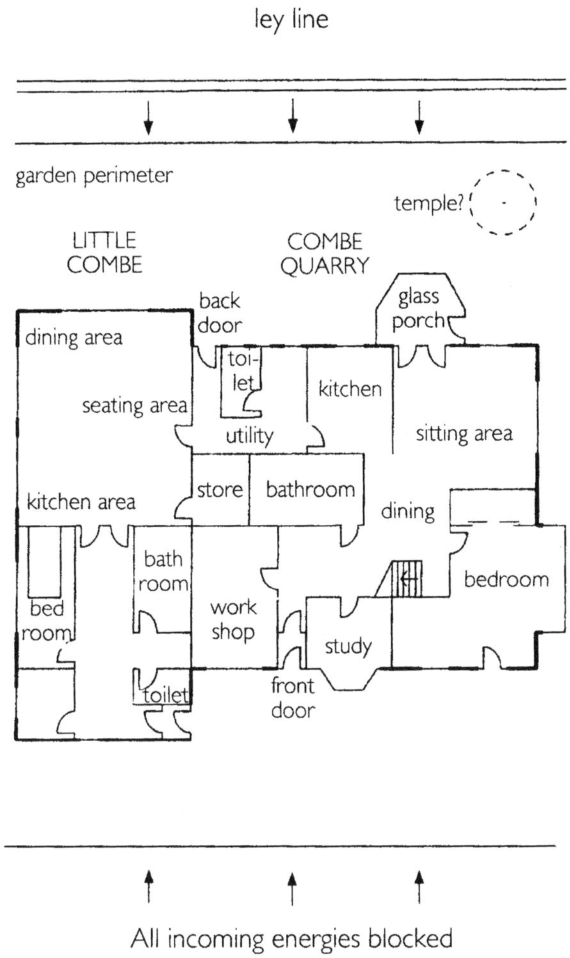

Plan of Little Combe and Combe Quarry

surprising, both in what you find and in how you can alter the lives of the people who are affected; at their request and for their benefit always.

12
Right and Left Brain Functions

Sometimes when we are trying to make a decision, we say that we are in 'two minds' about it. We also try to 'make up' our mind. And truly there seems to be two separate minds, the one rational, logical, sensible and practical, and the other impulsive and intuitive, making decisions which have little to do with common sense. We have a 'hunch' about something or 'an absurd notion' to do this or that.

Whether we have two minds or not, we certainly seem to have two brains, the right and the left hemispheres of what we call our brain, joined together by a great bridge of fibres and nerve cells called the corpus callosum. This contains over two million nerve cells and nerve fibres. By this means communication between the hemispheres can take place and one part of the brain can exchange information with another.

On the physical level each hemisphere directs most of the activity of the other side of the body; the left hemisphere controls movements of the right side of the body and the right hemisphere the left. So both sides of the brain are similar as far as motor functions are concerned.

They differ however in other respects. The left hemisphere is rather like a digital computer. Language and mathematics are both left hemisphere activities and these depend on linear time. The right hemisphere is more holistic and relational and simultaneous in the way that it works. It can perhaps be compared to a more advanced computer and can process a whole range of data simultaneously. It is responsible for space orientation, recognition of places and faces, body image and artistic endeavour.

How do we know all this? By various ways. The key was perhaps given when work was done on brain damaged people, those damaged at birth, by accident, or by the results of operation following status epilepticus (epileptic fits). In the latter it was found that if the corpus callosum was divided, two things happened; firstly the fits stopped, so that in one sense the operation could be called a success, and secondly the two halves of the brain seemed to produce two conscious entities or minds running in parallel in the same cranium, each with its own sensations, perceptions, learning experiences, memory and so on.

Quoting from Dr. Michael Gazzaniga: 'Each hemisphere is endowed with certain capacities that are either lacking or poorly represented in the other half-brain. For example, speech, analytical thought and logical reasoning originate in the left brains of most people and abstract thought, imagery, emotions and instincts seem to come from the right side of our head. But each brain serves as a backup system to the other and can take over most of its duties if the other half is injured.'

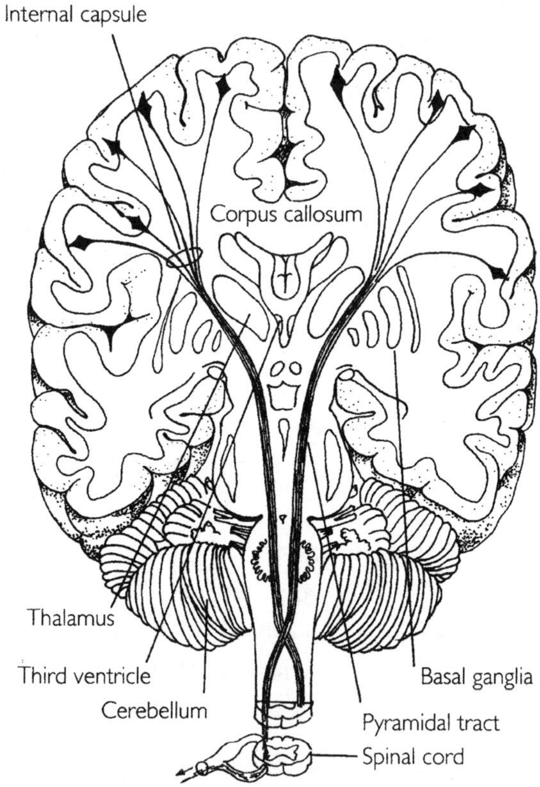

Cross section of brain

Most, but not all, as the epileptics after operation showed. Motor function of the body was maintained, the left hemisphere could still send instructions to the right side of the body and vice versa. But although the day to day working of the mind seemed to be unaffected, things like recognition of faces and spatial position were altered. These had to be re-learnt in left-brain terms. In this way the patient was restricted, rather like someone with dyslexia, who is unable to recognise letters and arrange them in spatial form to make words meaningful to himself.

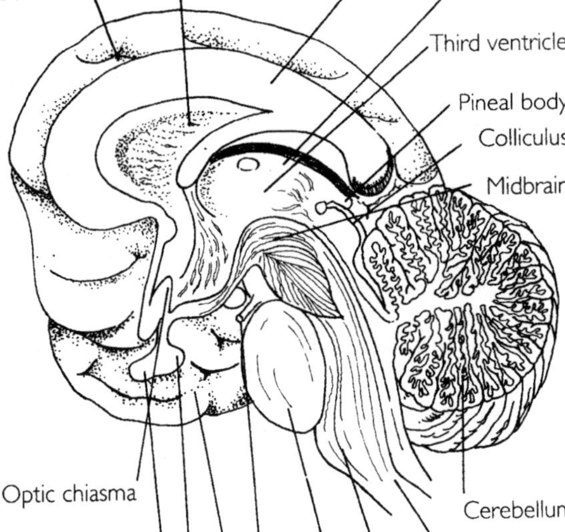

Section through midline of brain

If the two parts of the brain act differently when separated then they conceivably do the same when not separated, although each hemisphere will exercise control over the other. And so it seems they do. It appears also that one hemisphere is more dominant than the other and in our present state of civilization it is the left brain that dominates.

It seems reasonable therefore to think in terms of left mindedness and right mindedness, remembering that we normally use both halves but use the left half more than the right half.

Left brain	*Right brain*
Logical	Intuitive
Analytic	Holistic
Verbal	Visual
Objective	Subjective
Calculating	Dreaming
Practical	Creative
Rational	Irrational
Steady	Impulsive

Both right and left minded extremists are ridiculous. Those with a heavy predominance of the right mind spend their lives communicating with spirits, seeing visions, living in flights of fancy and continually in touch with the extraterrestrials and the unknown. The extremes of the left minded are intolerant of the creative impulse, sarcastically rational, logical to the extremity of nonsense, just as silly but considerably less entertaining.

Most people equate with some aspect of each hemisphere and show balance between the two halves of the brain. Within the normal range, some people are more left minded than right minded and others the reverse. A bank clerk, for instance, who catches the same train to work every morning, sits in the same carriage with the same paper, same conversation, acts strictly according to the rules and leads an ordinary useful non-exciting life can be said to be predominantly left minded. On the other hand a Madame Arcana who lives in a tiny little cottage amidst a jungle of weeds, dressing despite her age in brightly coloured veils and amulets; who spends much time receiving messages from the dead, forgetting to eat, utterly absentminded; perhaps she could be termed a predominantly right minded subject.

Sadly for such people the left minded types predominate and the right minded are often despised, hounded and persecuted. In pre-literate times, the right mind was more dominant, accepting as natural concepts the divine nature of the world and communicating through the shaman or priest with the otherworld. These people though illiterate were creative artists, intuitive and instinctive. They had a finely developed telepathic sense. With the spread of literacy to the ordinary man the left side of the brain became more and more dominant and a point was reached where instincts and so-called illusions were suppressed and regarded as witchcraft and superstition.

Our modern methods of education are almost wholly left mind orientated. It is interesting to speculate what might eventually happen. With the advent of computers and calculators the left mind is being used less and less by the average man. After all we have instruments to do things like calculating and manual skills. Parts of the body that are not used tend to atrophy. Perhaps in time the right brain function will become more and more evident. Perhaps this is already happening.

Much of what we are talking about today was known long ago. Speaking of hypnosis in 1889 it was said that 'the reasonable and deliberative side (of the brain) is developed and in proportion as the latter is predominant the greater generally is the success of the treatment.' The hypnotist then suggests that he is using his power to produce hypnotic trance by suppressing or bypassing the left hemisphere so that he can communicate directly with the right side of the mind.

Dr. David Pederson, President of the Society of Medical and

Dental Hypnosis, said in 1982, 'When we hypnotise a patient what we are doing is altering their mode of consciousness to the right hemisphere by inhibition of the left.' This could be shown by the high susceptibility to hypnosis of children and art students as compared with old people, science students and schizophrenics. Pederson found also that dreams can either be suppressed or induced by interfering with the right hemisphere.

As in hypnosis, in relaxation and meditative techniques the aim is to achieve deep relaxed attention. In this state the subject can experience, in a non-trance condition, predominately right brain functions which can lead to transformations in consciousness and functional efficiency. If one can visualize improved performance while in a deeply relaxed state then the visualisation will become a reality at the physical level. The mind/body link is the key to transcendent performance. This brings us into the area of healing energies. So, if the left brain is suppressed or diverted, apparently miraculous events can occur. Interestingly enough, in these states the electroencephalographic tracings of the brain alter, showing that the right hemisphere is predominant.

The right brain and the right mind are just as conscious as those of the left, but we can think of these areas as a sort of antechamber to the unconscious, a door perhaps which is normally very hard to open but which opens easily in hypnotic trance or meditative states. The unconscious is only termed the unconscious because we have no conscious appreciation of what it is doing. It is not inactive and is working all the time. When the left hemisphere is sleeping the unconscious is busy clearing up the mental rubbish of the day, solving problems, piecing things together, working out concepts. It keeps the body in trim in its day to day running. It remains on the alert and in a protective capacity.

Once the right mind has been told what to do, it will do it unless prevented by the left mind. To carry out a task beyond the normal it must be given specific instructions. When we are in left-minded sleep we obey orders without question and theoretically we can be made to do anything that is possible. In the case of left-handedness; the left hand is guided by the right brain. This is the hemisphere which specializes in perception of form and spacial relationships. Left-handed people are better at one-handed sports such as tennis. Einstein made full use of his right mind. He is said to have thought in images and would close his eyes to let the figures 'dance'. Gauss once exclaimed, 'I have the result, now let me see how I have arrived at it.'

To sum up

The Left Brain. This is the dimension of physical reality where life is experienced in physical terms and governed by known physical laws. These are experienced in linear terms, day follows night, death follows life. It is the realm of the finite and is bounded by restrictions and conditioned by beliefs.

The Right Brain. This is an area of consciousness outside of time and not conditioned by time. It is completely supportive and is a reservoir of creative forces which are available at all times and are not tied or bound by the physical body. From this dimension comes the energy and power that sustains the left brain and as a result, the physical body. There is no limit to what can be done. It is a bank of infinite information. What knowledge we need can be obtained. The simplest to the most complex desires become visualised. Only our beliefs can limit us and shape our physical experience. So in the right brain the source energies from which we form all events are present and from this dimension we draw on the events that make up our life according to our personal beliefs, desires and intents and possess unlimited power and potential. We set up contacts and circuits with other people in the right brain state which often appear as chance encounters or coincidence. There is no such thing as coincidence. We create our own reality.

13
Crystals and the Human Subtle Energy System

In recent years our knowledge of crystals has been reawakened and their ability to transmute and transform electromagnetic energies has resulted in great advances in technology. Crystals are beginning to give us the power to manipulate and transform knowledge and are now widely used in industry. In the 1960s a ruby was built into the first laser model. At a later date niobate crystals began to be used to store three dimensional holograms and large amounts of data can now be stored in this way. Minute natural quartz crystals are used to power watches and the production of pure artificial crystals of silicon has enabled scientists to harness another type of energy from the sun.

The use of crystalline technology is not new. We are told that in the ancient continent of Atlantis, which is said to have existed from 150,000 BC to 10,000 BC, crystals were used in this way to the degree that they appear to have caused the disruption of the continent. There seem to have been two manmade cataclysmic events which reduced Atlantis to a number of small islands before its final destruction in 10,000 BC.

The people of Atlantis seem to have been a mainly agricultural society gradually evolving over a period of time to advanced levels of society and culture, much as our own civilization has done. During the last 30,000 years of the continent's existence, technology and science had evolved to a very high degree. The Atlanteans were skilled in architectural engineering, astronomy, agriculture and especially in healing. Their technology was based on the higher dimensional energies of consciousness and the manipulation of subtle energy. For example they knew how to transform the energy of seeds into useable power for commerce and industry. It is thought that healing with the chakra powers of plants and gems was used widely. As today there were a great many stress-related disorders, and homoeopathic medicines and flower remedies were developed to treat such illnesses.

Much of the sophisticated Atlantean technology was said to be based on the energy production of crystals, particularly of the quartz crystal. These are capable of transmuting the sun's energy into utilizable power and broadcasting it to a distance. The therapeutic values of the crystal were also employed by passing sunlight through a crystal directly on to the patient in the same way that present day treatment is given by X-rays.

During the later stages of technological development it was thought that the tuning of individual crystals was too high and that because of this artificial balance of energies, major earthquakes occurred which contributed to the final destruction of Atlantis.

There seem to have been two factions in Atlantis: one

more spiritually directed, believing in the unity of life and the God-force; and the other very materialistic and concerned with the pleasures of life and with power. This second group used the technologies that were discovered, for materialistic gain and for destruction. They misused the knowledge of genetic engineering to create a race of mutant workers which they used as slave labour.

Towards the end of Atlantis there was civil war and the great sun crystals were abused and shattered. The final cataclysm came in 9600 BC. and the island sank. Before this date however groups of the more spiritual peoples of Atlantis had left and settled in the northern lands of the Atlantic, in Egypt, northern Europe, in the north of South America, in Yucatan and in Peru, carrying with them recorded crystals and other aspects of technology for the future. The people who were left behind perished.

We are now believed to be on the verge of discovering the holographic records of Atlantis and our technology is such that we may be able to decipher the encoded knowledge. We are also facing similar divisions in our society. Hopefully we shall not make the same mistakes as our predecessors.

The inner structure of a natural crystal shows a state of perfection and balance. It is able to emit vibrations which may affect a wide area and it can extend and amplify the mind of the user. Like a laser beam, it radiates energy in a highly concentrated form and we can use this energy in many ways. We are only now beginning to realize that like the animal and plant kingdoms, the mineral kingdom has awareness, although not necessarily on the same level. With awareness comes free will but this is not true of minerals which are largely dependent on the will of others, having little free will of their own. Crystals are however affected by higher will and are thus very powerful in combination with the user. Because they are so powerful they should only be used through the individual user's higher consciousness.

When energy is passed through a crystal the energy becomes transformed into a balance of physical and spiritual. It is this ability of crystals to transform and harmonize energies at all levels that is their greatest value and potential for use. The crystal does not increase the energy of the user but it focuses and balances it.

In some cases it adds to it because through the elemental of the crystal we can draw in an additional elemental energy that is in harmony with our own.

Just as every human being or animal has its individual energy, so has each crystal and so is each crystal different from others of its kind. We find that crystals located in one part of the earths surface vary considerably in their subtle energies from otherwise seemingly identical crystals found in another area.

In the Atlantean age, the Earth was beginning to reach fulfilment as a place where the consciousness of man was implanting the essence of spirit into the dense matter of the earth. Crystals were widely used for this purpose. Every crystal in the universe resounded to the higher energies that man was using through them. The ripples of both harmony and disharmony spread far beyond the planet.

Larger crystals were used at points where the major lines of earth power crossed, and the major spiritual centres which are now coming into being are located at these crossing points in the energy grid. Much of the crystal which was withdrawn from the Earth when Atlantis sank is now being returned and fed into this grid.

The mineral kingdom has both exoteric and esoteric elements in common with all other kingdoms of nature. The physical or material aspect is expressed through the many types, sizes and shapes in which crystalline growth may appear in nature. The spiritual aspect of crystals is seen in the inner geometric formation which is expressed as crystalline form. This is the manifestation of the underlying consciousness. All life and matter is governed by unseen laws of form and the crystal is perhaps the most perfect example of these laws. Within its structure the repeating geometric patterns and shapes give expression to the crystal energies within.

Each of the seven crystalline systems has a resonance with a particular subplane of energy in the mineral kingdom. The physical atomic pattern of the crystal may be compared with the patterning in the human etheric body which precedes the manifestation of cellular activity and cellular organisation in our physical body.

As the crystal grows in size, its atoms migrate into the appropriate position as guided by its etheric energy. When atoms of a like consciousness come together in the form of a crystal, a body of vibration energy with a definite vibration pattern is created.

Each of the seven subplanes of the mineral kingdom has a correspondence to the energies of a particular chakra in the human form. All crystals of the same system normally resonate with that chakra and affect it.

We should think of crystals as a solidified form of light

and energy. They generate and reflect electromagnetic energy and it is the play of this upon our own energy fields which brings about the effect.

The energy of a crystal is very cold and may be felt as coldne ss or tingling. Crystals draw all our weaknesses to the surface and we must work on these as they appear. Sometimes the emotions well up and it is not uncommon to see people weeping as they hold the crystal; it is better to allow the emotions to surface rather than hold them back.

Choosing a Crystal for Yourself

A crystal, your crystal, is a very personal possession. Always choose your own, choose for yourself... the choice you will realise is not entirely yours, for a crystal chooses you for its own work.

Given an array of crystals you will feel drawn to one of them, not necessary the most beautiful. You pick it up, then put it down and look at others, but eventually you are back with your first choice.

A crystal comes to you for a specific purpose. Once you begin to work with it, it will accelerate your personal development. Memories of past lives may begin to surface; you may become emotional or have other feelings. To check whether the crystal is right for you, hold it in your hand over your heart chakra. A positive reaction is a feeling of cold energy coming from the stone. If after a short time there is no reaction, proceed to do the same with the other chakra points. If these do not react also, the crystal is not for you. Pick another one.

Cleansing and Programming a Crystal

Next, cleanse your crystal. It is important to do this from time to time. Energies from other people have accumulated in it since it was mined. You neither want or need these. It is enough that the natural energies remain.

Wash your crystal in flowing water, cool or cold. Holding the crystal in the water, will that undesirable energies be washed away and that the desirable ones remain. Ask the elementals of the water to accept the negative energy and transform it into positive energy. And thank them for doing so.

Sunlight is a great cleanser, so expose the crystal to the sun for a few hours. Some crystals seem to prefer to be buried in the earth and cleansed in this way. Your own intuition will tell you. Depending on the use your crystal is put to, it may require cleansing frequently. If, for example, it is used for healing, cleansing between each healing is necessary.

Now, programme your crystal. Programming is the process of instructing the elemental of the crystal to use its ability to transform balance and negativity. Programming is by intent and this is perhaps the best way to put in the programme. Tell it what you wish it to do. Once a crystal has been programmed for a specific use, do not use it for other purposes or the original programme will be cancelled. The use of crystals requires a real clarity of purpose and one must plan each move in advance.

As we become more aware and more awake spiritually and as our own particular vibrations change, different crystals come into our lives to correspond and harmonize with these vibrations. The first point of contact with crystal energies may be made through meditation. In meditation we are able to reach higher and higher levels as the crystal focuses the energy. Holding a crystal during meditation liberates the energy. This energy may often be seen as colour.

Crystals in Healing

One major area in which crystals are used is healing. The essence of healing is energy transference, causing a change in the auric and higher energies which is ultimately reflected in the physical body. As healing takes place harmony is restored to the subtle bodies, and this is the major function of the crystal when used in this way. Even if there is no physical disease present in the body there is still benefit, because the crystal cleanses and balances the aura.

Certain types of injury to the body, particularly those involving bone structure, cause disturbances of the body's energy field that last longer than other injuries. Bone has a crystalline structure and the pain and injury tend to programme themselves into the structure. Energy transference from the crystal occurs because of resonance between the crystal and the crystalline system of the bone cells. Quartz should be programmed with the intention of drawing the disharmonious programme from the bone and replacing it with a programme designed to promote healing of the tissue.

Crystals are important in reducing shock and pain in any part of the body. They allow the natural healing processes to take place. They supplement whatever technique the healer uses. Because they are thought energy amplifiers, the thought directed energies of the healer are intensified and at the same time broadcast to some distance. This is the basis of distant healing. The clearer the thought or the image held by the healer the more accurate the information held by the crystal. The energy mechanism of the crystal, however, can only accept one lot of information at a time, so that it must be cleared or cleansed before putting in a second programme.

The quartz crystal is most commonly used in crystal healing. It belongs to the hexagonal tetrahedral system, and is probably the most easily recognised crystal in the group. Quartz is formed all over the world where there has been volcanic action. The crystals are composed of silicon dioxide and have their greatest potential in their effect on the subtle energies. They respond to a wide spectrum of energies; heat, light, pressure, sound, electricity, and even the energies of consciousness.

In response to these energies the molecular structure of the crystal will cause specific frequencies of energy emission. Each variety of quartz has its own special energy and properties. The colours of the other crystals in the family are given by trace elements. Amethyst, for example, has the trace element manganese, giving its violet colour. Amethysts have a natural ability to draw negative energies from their surroundings. They can be used as 'spiritual room fresheners'.

It is not possible in a book of this type to give more than a brief outline of crystals and their properties, or more detailed information about each group or family of crystals. This is a very large subject and you are referred to the booklist for further information. All the books suggested are eminently readable and there are excellent courses available if you wish to take the subject further.

14
Flower and Gem Essences

EDWARD BACH was born in Birmingham at the end of the nineteenth century.

From childhood he showed a great compassion for everything that suffered; humans, plants, animals, anything in distress aroused in him the desire to help and to heal. He determined from a very early age that he would find a simple method of healing that was a cure for all ills and began to study the methods of healing available to him. Torn between a career in either the church or the medical profession, he chose medicine. He reasoned that by observing and treating the sick on the wards he would begin to understand the real differences between illness and health and as he watched the patients in his care he became aware that the same drug could be given to two people with the same medical condition and it might cure one but not the other. It seemed that the personality, the character of the patient had very much to do with his reaction to the prescribed drug. He noted that in two people with identical illness, the one dreamy and inactive, the other, active and impatient, a different drug for each patient could restore his normal health.

Bach was by now a qualified doctor and his work load was much greater. In spite of this he still made copious notes on all the people that he treated. He observed that in an illness the process of healing was often very painful and involved suffering for the patient. True healing, he said, should not involve pain, it should be gentle and benign, without harmful side effects. He saw much chronic disease for which there was no cure and he felt that he should be able to find some answer to these problems. This led him into the study of immunology – the ability of the body to produce its own resistance to disease.

About this time he became very ill himself and decided that if he had not long to live he must try to leave as much information as possible for those who followed him. He returned to work and became so absorbed in what he was doing that he forgot his illness altogether. In his notes he made the observation that patients had a better chance of survival in an illness if they kept working than if they gave up and retired to bed.

Bach's interests now turned towards homoeopathic medicine. He moved to the London Homoeopathic Hospital as a consultant. Continuing his research into illness he found that when a drug was given in homoeopathic dosage, adverse reaction to that drug was either diminished or absent.

It was at this time that he described the seven nosodes. These were substances produced from the patient's own disease which were then used in homoeopathic doses to stimulate the resistance of the body to that particular disease. Using this method he was able to cure many formerly untreatable illnesses. (These nosodes are still in use in homoeopathy and are known as the Seven Bach Nosodes.)

There seemed no simple method by which disease could be treated, and Dr Bach became very depressed. He could find no answer to his problems. There should be something, somewhere, which carried the positive energies of health, but everything that he tried failed.

One evening, at a big dinner party, his mind wandering as usual, the answer came. It suddenly occurred to him that people could be divided into groups according to the way they talked, the way they behaved, ate their food, and so on. In their basic responses different people in a group could be similar to one another. On reaching home he tried to work out all the possible different types of people and the categories in which they could be placed according to their behaviour patterns. Working on this basis he developed the first three of the remedies which now form part of the Bach system. He potentised the remedies by homoeopathic methods and tried them out on his patients. In 1928, delighted with his results, he gave up his very lucrative practice in London, determined to spend the rest of his life in research on the remedies, considering them to be the positive qualities able to counteract disease in the patient. He tested many remedies and set standards for them. They must be non-poisonous and do no harm to the body. He decided that the first remedies must be made from plants which grew at the height of summer when the sun was at its strongest. He knew already that there were many plants in use which relieved suffering, many of them described in herbals, but he was looking for plants which produced a harmonising of the whole being. Slowly he developed the first twelve of his remedies. From that time they were the only remedies that he used. The twelve remedies were based on twelve states of emotion which are common to all people. They were completely harmless and brought in healing.

At this point he ran into trouble with the General Medical Council. His methods were unacceptable; he advertised, so that healing could be available to all those who wanted it, and he made his remedies available without prescription; all very heinous sins.

But it didn't stop Bach. Having determined that different people reacted in different ways to the same remedy, he saw a link between this and homoeopathy. (His basic reasoning was that, for example, five people might have a cold but each will have a different sort of cold, one may be shivery, one very hot, one with a running nose, another with a stuffy nose, another with a sore throat, and so on. None of us reacts in the same way to an illness; one of us may be irritable, one impatient, one very sorry for himself.) As Edward Bach watched the different types of people and their varied reaction to illness he decided that each type of reaction related to different bacteria which were present in the body. It seemed to him that patients with certain characteristics were liable to suffer from certain bacteria. He claimed to be able to recognise the organism affecting the patient by his behaviour. This method is still used in homoeopathy, diagnosis is based on general appearance, the colour of the skin, the way that the patient moves and responds rather than the actual symptoms.

Dr Bach had moved a long way towards the homoeopathic methods of diagnosis. He tried above all to find a method of healing people, which, unlike homoeopathy, did not use any poisonous substances. Homoeopaths use remedies that in the raw state can cause a similar reaction to the one suffered by the patient. This may be a poison. Belladonna, for example is a poisonous plant but if diluted homoeopathically it can be used to treat symptoms such as dilated pupils, fever, and delirium which are similar to those found in belladonna poisoning. Bach did not agree with this; he tried to find a way of treatment which was very simple, very pure, easy to apply and free from any irritating factors.

Our present thinking is that unless the physical body is in harmony with the subtle bodies, we lay ourselves open to infections and other illnesses. We know that how we think and how we feel is important and that for true health, the lower levels of our being must be in harmony with the higher vibrations. It would seem that if we can treat disease on the level of the aura before it becomes manifest as disease in the body, we might have the answer to healing in very simple terms. By treating the precursors of disease in the emotional and mental areas, in the moods of our patients we have a very good chance of effecting a healing.

There are thirty-eight Bach Remedies and they are all used for emotional states, thirty-nine if we include the Rescue Remedy which is used as a sort of first aid treatment in situations where the emotions are concerned, such as shock, after an accident or perhaps a sudden death in the family or a similar situation. Bach divided the thirty-eight into groups of seven main types of moods: fear, loneliness, uncertainty, despair, despondency, over-concern for others, and those people who lack interest in life. All the remedies have different manifestations. Taking the ones for fear as an example, there are:

Mimulus, for nervous timid fear. Someone who is scared of everything, scared of flying, of dogs, cats, or of something that might hurt them.

Rock rose is a panic remedy.

Aspen, a general state of anxiety. Nebulous unknown fears. Often associated with religious phobias.

Cherry plum. This is for desperation. It is the one to use if someone is suicidal; if they have a fear of losing control, losing sanity. Fear of being pushed beyond the limit.

Red chestnut; this is connected with fear for other people, for example, the parent who lies awake at night, waiting for the child to come home and fearing the worst.

Gorse is also a remedy relating to great despair. One just gives up, there is nothing to live for.

Scleranthus is a remedy used for uncertainty. It is often useful in cases of travel sickness.

Vine for a very strong forceful and determined person who is afraid.

The Bach remedies work to balance those states of mind When put into the mouth they are absorbed straight into the nervous system without passing through the gut as does food. In this way they are linked strongly with the mind and the subtle bodies.

Remedies have both a positive and negative action. For example, Clematis in its negative quality is useful for a person who daydreams and is not down to earth, is not really aware of what is going on around them. Clematis helps the earthing. The positive side is for a person who is aware on the higher levels, highly intuitive, expressing a great deal of sensitivity and because of this is unduly exposed to the world. This type of person may become very negative and find life very difficult.

Children and animals respond very quickly to the remedies, perhaps because they are natural and uncomplicated. It is suggested that perhaps, when treating adults we should try to envisage them as children, when they showed their real and not imagined fears and joys.

The Preparation of Flower Remedies

You will need:

A large glass bowl big enough to hold twelve ounces or the equivalent of water

Glass bottles and a pouring funnel

Non-carbonated distilled water. Do not use spring water because the flower remedies pick up any pollution in the water

The flowers are picked just before maturity and only the healthiest flowers are picked. Flowers from the sunny side of the plant are the more potent. The blooms are floated on the top of the water and the bowl should stand in the sun close to the parent plant for two to three hours. This is called the Mother Essence. Pour this into a large clean bottle which is half filled with brandy.

From the mother essence the stock bottles are made. Each bottle of stock remedy should contain seven drops of mother essence to one fluid ounce of water. From this the remedy for the patient can be made. This contains 3-5 drops of the stock essence to a fluid ounce of distilled water.

Gem Remedies are made in a similar manner. The mineral should be a natural one, not a cut or tumbled stone. All bowls etc. should be made of glass. The stone should be cleansed in the usual way, by putting it in the sun or in a solution of sea salt. It is then placed in a bowl of water and put in the sun on a wooden or glass base. Potency is helped by putting quartz crystals around the bowl and sitting in meditation for a few minutes. After about two hours, remove the stone and pour the fluid into a storage bottle. Spring is the best time to prepare the remedy.

Homoeopathic Remedies differ from flower and gem remedies in that they are usually made from denser materials and function mainly on the level of the physical body. They often duplicate the vibrations of physical disease in order to rebalance the body. Flower remedies act on the subtle bodies and the etheric levels and influence the physical body at this level. Gem remedies act between the two. If the stones are crushed or powdered they act more as homoeopathic remedies but when a gem is prepared as an elixir (see above), the remedy acts more like a flower essence. Gems influence specific organs in the body and homoeopathic remedies are more general in their influence. It is unwise to give too many gem or homoeopathic remedies at the same time as this may worsen the condition. Flower remedies however can be combined and as many as six to eight may be taken at the same time.

Homoeopathic and gem essences are best taken by mouth. Flower remedies are most effective when put into a warm bath. The three types of remedy should not be taken at the same time.

Each type of remedy has certain difficulties. Physical

problems can block the actions of flower remedies but the effects are self-adjusting. Similarly gem elixirs may produce a mild healing crisis which also adjusts in time. With too little gem remedy the effects are weak and this does not help the condition. Whilst flower remedies may affect the etheric body as well as the physical body, gem remedies do not have as much life essence as flowers and primarily influence the physical.

Too much homoeopathic remedy may give complications and problems; too little and the crystalline structures of the body are not activated because there is not a great deal of life force in these remedies.

For a beginner, flower remedies are the safest to use because they have no side effects; but as the emotional blocks are removed, there may be points of confrontation. The underlying nature of the person treated may emerge. Not all of us are very nice within. So go carefully, too little rather than too much and don't be too hasty in your treatment.

In the sixty years or so that Edward Bach first produced his remedies, the world has changed. Our consciousness is awakening, our own rates of vibration have changed and it is time now to find other remedies to heal and help our progress on levels other than purely physical and emotional.

Other flower essences, gem elixirs and star remedies have become available and it seems as though we are having to work in a different area, in a different way. We are working more on the etheric, undoing blockages to unconditional love, trying to attune the body holistically and so on, and this means working with higher frequencies and increasingly subtle energies.

Examples of these more readily available remedies include:

Gem elixirs. These balance the vibrations and subtle energies of the body, the emotional, psychological and spiritual levels and this leads to balance of the physical.

Desert flower essences. Encourage self-awareness through union with nature.

Australian bush essences. Bring clarity to the conscious mind and help to resolve negative beliefs.

Chakra essences. These act directly on the chakras, balancing and unblocking them.

Don't buy them all! See if you feel drawn to any of the essences. Test them with your pendulum or in other ways. Enjoy yourself!

15
The Eyes Have It

We should think of the eyes as an optical instrument built into the body; vital for everyday performance and an instrument par excellence; sturdy, reliable and accurate. The eyes take in the rays of light and pick out the individual rates of colour but it is the brain that does the work of receiving and interpreting the train of electrical impulses from the eyes, reversing the picture because the picture received is upside down and adjusting for distance so that we have a three dimensional view. This last is particularly clever; the right eye has a different view from the left and this gives us the three dimensional quality.

And there is more! For the eye is a very subtle instrument. The central part registers detail and colour in daylight and the outer areas are adapted for seeing in the dark. B-Carotene is the chief ingredient in the visual purple found in the rods in the retina and it is this that enables us to have night vision. Perhaps you can remember being told that you must eat carrots so that you can see in the dark! And I believed it.

Carrot sales were high in my childhood.

The development of the human eye has taken hundreds and thousands of years of trial and error, a gradual refinement of vision so that we can now see what we see. We need not think that development of the eye has stopped.

The radiation that we call light covers only a tiny band of the electromagnetic spectrum but we are able to detect and colour code the different wavelengths in this band; the longer wavelengths which are reflected in the autumn leaves in the woodlands appearing as reds and oranges and the shorter wavelengths, the greens and the blues which we can see in the sky and in water. We rely on these vibrations of light for information about our surroundings and as a result our eyesight is very well developed.

The eyes of animals and fish are sensitive to other wave bands and many insects, fish and birds can see beyond blue to the ultraviolet band, which we cannot see.

Shorter wavelengths can damage an animal's eyes just as ultraviolet can damage our own. Even the band of wavelengths which we share with animals can give a very different impression to animal or man because there are a wide variety of eye designs in the natural world. Birds have eyes very like our own but some birds are able to enhance the image in the middle of the field, a sort of telephoto lens. These are mainly predators and use this ability to find prey. Others can see a far greater range of colour than we can see. One reason that we have an advantage over many animals is because our brain receives information about wavelength and brightness hitting the eye and converts this into a multicoloured three dimensional image. Much of our brain is directed to sight and this is not so in other animals who although they have similar eyes have not the brain development of man.

The simplest true eyes are cup shaped and lined with photosensitive cells. The opening of the cup is narrowed and shows a crude image like that of a pinhole camera. When the hole is small there is a fairly clear image and many small creatures such as slugs and snails can function with this, but if the opening is any bigger, such as we have in our own eyes, a lens is necessary to bend the rays of light so that they can fix on one point.

The eyes of all vertebrates have a similar design. Again the eye acts rather like a camera. The transparent window at the front of the eye, the cornea, bends and refracts light as it enters the eye. Behind this is an area called the iris. This is the pigmented area which determines for us the colour of the eye. The rays pass

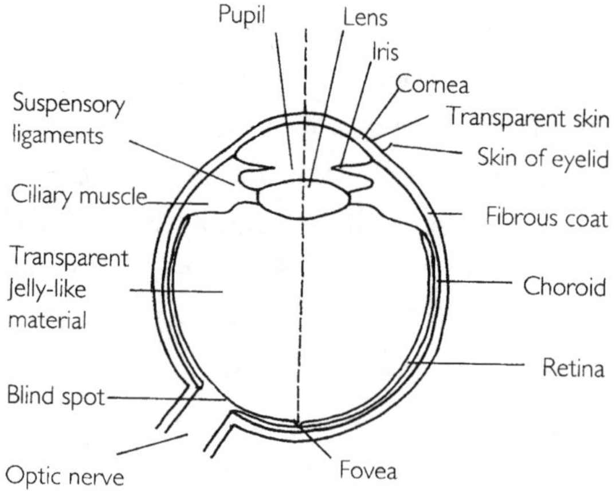

The eye of a mammal

through a hole in the iris to the lens, which is curved, and the lens project the light on the retina which is at the back of the eye. Muscles attached to the lens allow us to focus the eye by making it more rounded or flattening it.

The focused light strikes the retina which is made up of light detectors, rod and cone shaped. Each contains a photosensitive pigment and the change that this undergoes on exposure to light sends a signal via the optic nerve to the brain. Here the impulses are interpreted and the brain reverses the image and interprets it from previous experience.

In the very primitive vertebrates the brain has less involvement with sight and much visual information never

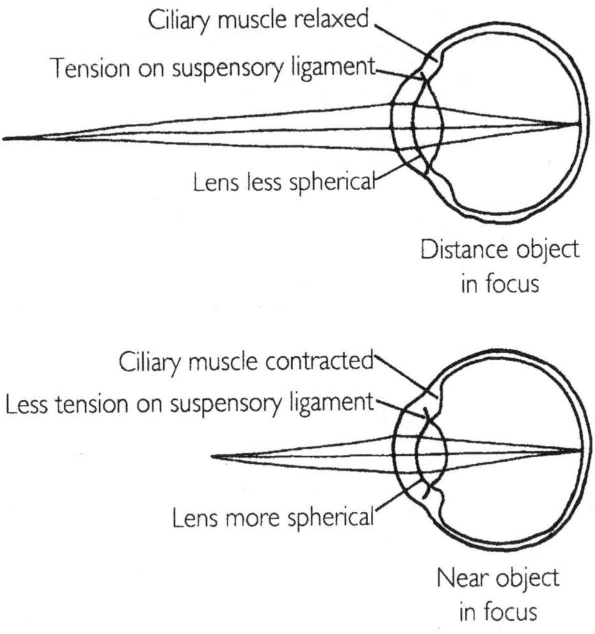

Section through a human eye

reaches it. In these creatures the light entering triggers automatic reactions.

Many invertebrates have not only smaller brains but they have eyes of a very different design from ours, often placed outside the head area.

The eyes of insects are made up of tiny hexagonal units. These are packed closely together to form a single unit but each one is able to act like an eye.

It records far less detail. In the different species of insects the numbers differ: the bee for instance has 5,000 units and the dragonfly has 30,000.

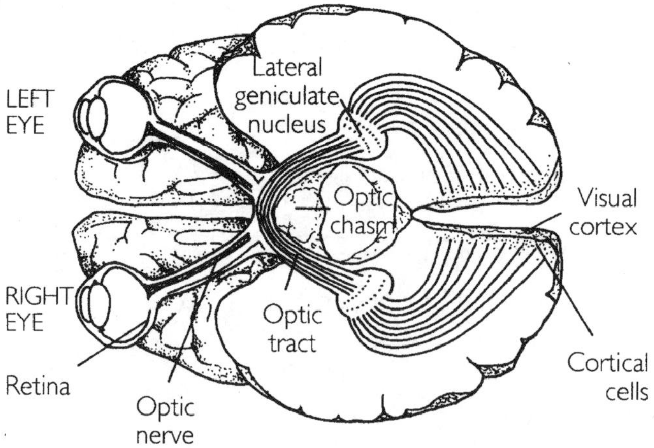

Cross section of brain showing optical tracts

Fine focusing of the eye is carried out by the lens which can be altered by the muscles attached to it. If the muscles relax the lens becomes rounded and objects near to us can be seen clearly. With contraction of the muscles the lens flattens and we are able to see distant objects in more detail. Large eyes are necessary to see fine detail; they have more light receptor units present.

Man is a predator and has his eyes situated at the front of the head; so has a cat, a fox, and a bird of prey. Animals that are prey have their eyes situated at the sides of the head so that they can see the predator coming.

We need two eyes to judge distance and the three dimensional image is produced by comparing two overlapping views.

Not every animal is able to see colour. Our brain colours the image, making the grass green and the sky blue. This involves the recognition and coding of the different wavelengths of light which reach us. The cones in the retina distinguish the different wavelengths which are interpreted as colours by the brain. The human brain receives information about red, green and blue light from the cones.

Primates, including man, can see these three colours and the monkey world sees colour as we do. Frogs also respond to similar colours but because their brains are not as specialised as ours the colours produce automatic reactions. In danger the frog will leap for the nearest batch of blue; usually water.

Some people lack one pigment usually red or green and are said to have colour blindness. These are usually men (4% of European men to 0.25% of women). Many other animals have the same absence of pigment and this may be seen particularly in dogs who cannot distinguish red from green.

Some fish have five colours in their eyes but the creatures that can see most colour are birds. As well as the pigments they have a filter mechanism and can distinguish more hues than we can. Each bird has cones and filter adapted to its needs but the sensitivity to red is common to all. Red flowers are pollinated by humming birds, red berries and fruit are used by plants to attract birds so that their seed is spread widely. Underwater animals and fish show more sensitivity to blue light. Red pigment is replaced by blue pigment. But in muddy waters where fish such as the pirana live, all but the red end of the spectrum of light is absorbed by the decaying vegetation. The eyes of that particular fish are adapted to red with horrid consequences!

Our retina is sensitive to ultraviolet light but the eye filters it out before it reaches and damages the light detectors. Other creatures, mainly insects, are able to use ultraviolet. Bees can see ultraviolet, and blue and green flowers have evolved an ultraviolet component to attract them. Some flowers have ultraviolet marks to guide the bee to the nectar. Equally some predators can change their colour to match the petals of the flowers.

Eyes adapted for seeing in the dark have to be protected from the light because they are ultrasensitive. Some of them, for example in the cat family, have pupils that become slits in bright light. In humans during day time the centre of the field is clear and the sides of the retina are not in use. Night vision relies mainly on the light receptors called rods and these are found mainly at the sides and at the periphery of the eye. This is the reason that when we walk in the dark we can see more clearly out of the sides of the eye.

In the next chapters we shall try to understand the effects of light upon the human body and then consider how we can use our knowledge of colour in healing.

16
MORE FACTS AND FIGURES

AT THIS POINT I would like to introduce some more detail. We are entering into the realms of light and sound and it is a difficult path to follow. Although ideally this information should appear at the end of this book, I have decided that it would be more helpful to put it here.

The complete spectrum of electromagnetic energy contains 60 to 70 octaves.

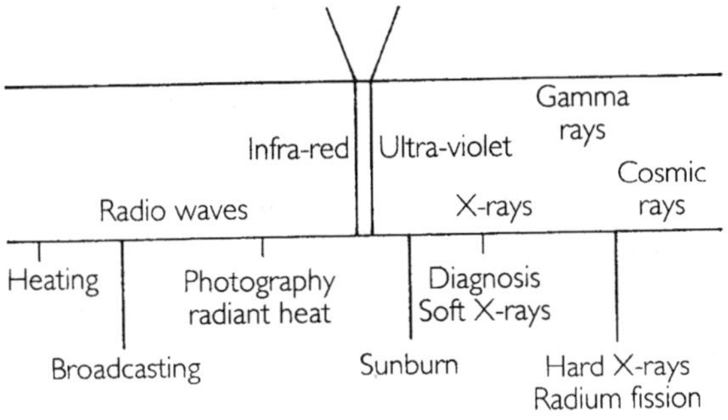

Wavelengths

Electromagnetic waves arise whenever an electric charge changes its velocity. Electrons moving from a higher to a lower energy level will radiate a wave of particular frequency and wavelength.

An electron possesses no measurable properties, no size, shape, area or volume. It can manifest as a particle or as a wave. It can also dissolve into a blurry cloud of energy and behave as if it were a wave of energy.

Light waves, gamma waves, radio waves and X-rays can change from waves to particles and back again. Because they can be both waves and particles they are termed quanta. The only time that electrons appear as particles is when we look at them. It has been said that when an electron is not being looked at it manifests as a wave.

Spectrum of electromagnetic energies

Octaves of electromagnetic energy at oscillatory frequencies	*Octave*
Form manifests	1 – 3
Sound	3 – 20
Highest note on the piano, 32/oscillations per second	12
Highest audible sound	15
All sound ceases	20
Heat (called dark light) is felt	45
Infrared (invisible) rays, the thermal spectrum of light	47 – 49
Colour is visible	49
Ultraviolet rays	50 – 56
Softest X-rays	57
Radium emanations	61
Magnetism	Over 18 billion million oscillations per sec

Light travels at a speed of 186,000 miles per second, too fast for the human eye to see. From the sun it spirals earthwards in concentric circles. Within the spectrum of white light lies colour. The colours of the spectrum are classified according to their wave length. They are given here in fractions of an inch and also in Angstrom units which are 1/10 millionth of a metre.

Wavelengths of Colour

Colour	*Inches*	*Angstrom units*
Red	1/33,000	8,000 – 7500
Orange	1/38,000	6,500
Yellow	1/43,000	6,000
Green	1/50,000	5,500
Blue	1/57,000	5,000
Indigo	1/59,000	4,500
Violet	1/65,000	4,000 – 3,800

Complementary Colours

When you look fixedly at a colour for about a minute and then look at a white or pale surface you will see another colour. This is called the complementary colour.. The colours and their complementary colours are as follows:

Red / turquoise
Orange / blue
Yellow / violet
Green / magenta
Turquoise / red
Blue / orange
Violet / yellow

This is more easy to follow when expressed as the Colour Circle or Colour Wheel.

The complementary colours are of great importance in colour therapy, both in their own right and in the avoidance of an overdose of the main therapy in treatment.

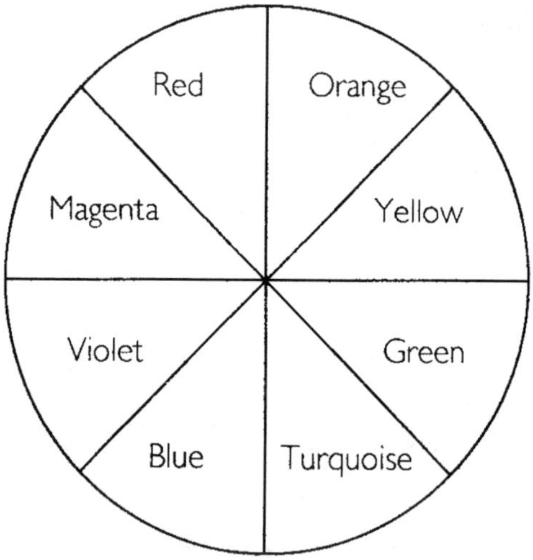

Colour Wheel

17
Light and the Human Body

LIGHT, FOR US, is the primal element of life. We cannot live in darkness and in the total absence of light we would die. It is a horrid thought!

Small wonder then that so much emphasis is given to the use of light in healing. From Greece and Rome we read that light was used for its preventive and curative effects, as it is today. Sunlight has been described as 'that superterrestrial natural force under which all life originates and develops'.

Our understanding of this great natural force has until recently been limited to observation. Towards the end of the nineteenth century when tuberculosis was a major cause of death in Britain it was observed that many patients improved when exposed to natural light. Many of the large sanatoria were built at this time, and the numbers of deaths from TB declined. Many other illnesses improved in similar ways. For example it had been known that babies with neo-natal jaundice cleared completely when exposed to sunlight, and this now became the treatment of choice.

Treatment by natural light was one of trial and error and it was not until the early part of this century that anything was known about the path of light once it has entered the body; even less was known about the effects of light upon the body as a whole. Since then and particularly in the last fifty years a very different picture has emerged.

Earlier in the last century various investigators found nerve fibres in the human body which were not present in the optic tract but which appeared to connect the eye with the region of the hypothalamus. Although these findings confirmed previous observations they were not accepted. Later work by Hendrickson (1972), Moore (1973), Hartwig (1974) and others proved conclusively that a pathway existed from the eyes to the hypothalamus. Early in 1935 Frey noted that the retinothalamic pathway was stimulated by light immediately after birth and that this function preceded the stimulation of the optic tract.

The major route of entry of light into the body is through the eyes. Here, the one hundred and thirty seven million photoreceptors (seven million cones and one hundred and thirty million rods) transform the physical stimulus of light into neurosensory impulses by photochemical reactions. The resulting electrical excitation runs along two different routes, one stimulating the visual area of the cortex and the other to the hypothalamus. Thus the optic tract conveys the visual stimuli to the visual cortex, enabling us to see and interpret what we have seen, and the second pathway to the hypothalamus energizes our vital functions.

So we may say that there is a nonvisual pathway from the retina which stimulates the *pineal* gland. This tiny gland, about the size of a pea, was thought until recently to be an atavistic remnant of the earlier development of man as a species. It had been noted in the past that it contained light-sensitive cells but no definite conclusions had been drawn. We now know that far from being an atavistic remnant, the pineal gland is a vital part of the endocrine system.

The pineal is highly active in humans when they are young and its secretion prevents the premature onset of puberty and the development of sexual functions. It effects this by

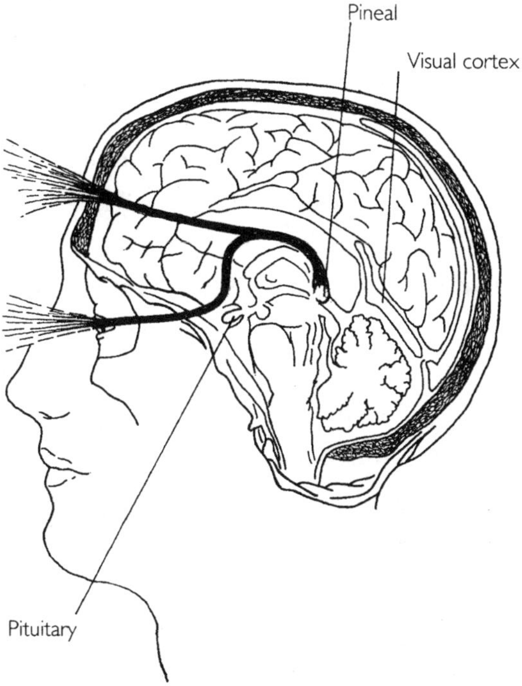

Non visual pathway from retina to pituitary and pineal

the release of a substance called *melatonin*, the secretion of which follows a regular daily rhythm. It is released in response to darkness, the highest release level being between two and three in the early morning. As the pineal gland is an endocrine gland it secretes directly into the surrounding medium, in this case the cerebrospinal fluid in which it is bathed. From here it affects both the hypothalamic part of the brain and the pituitary body.

The *hypothalamus* controls vital functions by both neural and endocrine routes. In this way it has control over energy balance, fluid balance, heat regulation activity and sleep, circulation and breathing, growth, maturation and reproduction through the sympathetic and parasympathetic systems and most of the glandular hormonal secretions through the pituitary gland. It is thus the main controller of our life processes.

The *pituitary* gland is also controlled by secretions from the pineal gland. It, the pituitary, has been called the master gland of the body, regulating as it does the secretions of all the endocrine glands. But the pineal can be described as a 'Regulator of regulators', for it affects reproductive function, growth, mood, blood pressure, body temperature, sleep, tumour growth, and the immune system. It also seems to be a factor in longevity.

Since the pineal gland, which is most active during the night, works in co-ordination with the pituitary, which is most active during the day, light entering the eyes acts as a synchronizer between these two photoneuro-endocrine glands.

We might then expect those people who are blind to have gross disturbance of function. Indeed they do. In 1971

Hollwich published a study on three hundred and sixty blind and one hundred and ten cataract patients before and after cataract surgery. He found that where light perception was absent or diminished or even, as in cataracts, temporarily disturbed, deficiencies occurred in both endocrine and metabolic systems as well as disturbances in emotional and physiological balance.

One is reminded here of Queen Victoria who 'did not wish to hear'. In those who do not wish to see there is a temporary shutdown and contraction of the visual fields which produces the same effects.

Light does of course enter the body in ways other than by the eyes. A small percentage enters by the skin. The ultra-violet part of the spectrum produces solitrol, a hormone believed to be part of Vitamen D3. This hormone works in conjunction with melatonin to control the body's responses to light and darkness and influences many of the body's regulatory centres as well as the hormone system.

A third, though not yet scientifically proven, route for light to enter the body is in the region of the *third eye*. Activation of the pineal body results. Whilst this is believed to occur in some animals, lizards and perhaps crocodiles, it is thought that little if any light enters by this route in man although at one time in man's development it may have done so.

Colour is merely our appreciation of light in different frequencies and it is logical that different colours might create different physiological as well as psychological effects on the body. The transpeduncular nucleus is the colour sensitive part of the brain; it responds to different frequencies of light, i.e. colour. It is now known that specific frequencies or wavelengths interact differently with the endocrine system to stimulate or inhibit hormonal production.

In 1958, Robert Gerard did a study for his doctorate on the effect of viewing coloured light on psychophysiological functions. Using blue, white and red light he showed that the visual cortex and the autonomic system were less aroused with blue and with white light than with red. He also showed that different coloured lights produce different feelings in the same subject. Blue stimulation was associated with an increase in relaxation, less anxiety and less subjective disturbance. The converse was true with red stimulation which produced tension, anger and increased physiological activation.

Wolfarth and Sam in 1982 not only confirmed the effect of selected colours on behaviour and physiology but found that blind people were as affected as sighted ones.

The human body does not only take in light but most if not all cells give out light at a very low level. In a recent paper by Edward et al. it is stated that the intensity of emission is one photon per cell in 3-20 minutes for mammalian cells which give off mainly the red end of the spectrum, that is to say, the light tends to be stronger at the red end rather than at the blue end of the spectrum. Much of the light is thought to be the result of free radicals during oxidative metabolism. But it is suggested that part of the light is generated by vibrations in the DNA. Emission of light may have considerable significance. If the theory of coherent patterned excitation is true, one might expect changes in light output when cells enter a disorganised state, as in cancer, and it is an interesting observation that energy emission over cancer tumours seems to be increased, but as heat rather than light, heat being at a lower vibration level.

The photon emission differs markedly between cancerous

and normal cells. Some kind of communication between cells has been suggested. There is also a general tendency for light output to increase to a maximum in the evening. No explanation is offered for this.

There are many imponderables, many things we cannot yet understand. That the body gives off light there can be no doubt. It is a small amount only and too faint to be perceived by the naked eye. The average fluxes for the body are one hundred photons per square centimetre per second. Experimentally the palm of the hand yields more light than any other part of the body. The average fluxes of visible protons per square centimetre are: hand, five hundred; forehead, three hundred; and trunk, one hundred.

A difference is found between old and young subjects. Older test subjects have twice the emission of light from the hands and three times that of younger subjects from the forehead.

Projecting Energy

The eye, as well as taking in energy as light, can project energy. Look fixedly across the room at someone who perhaps has his back to you. Defocus your eyes slightly. Deliberately project a beam of energy; that it does not appear as light does not matter. After a few moments your victim will start to be uneasy, anxious, shuffling about slightly and finally turning to look you directly in the face. Strange? Not really; anyone can do this. What are we sending? – perhaps it is not light but it is an electromagnetic energy of some kind. The snake fixes its eyes upon its victim, a mouse, and for some reason the mouse is unable to move. The stoat dances at the foot of a tree, its eyes fixed upon a bird and the bird watching falls from the tree to its predator. What is the energy that is sent? Perhaps this beam is light; we have no proof. But it does happen, and practice by the sender increases the ability to send.

There are higher reaches of light open to each one of us. The ability to see them is different for each of us because it depends on the level of the consciousness. This light is of extremely high frequency, many octaves higher than the light that we can perceive normally. To see this type of light requires the raising of one's own level of frequency, the level of one's own understanding, so that the two frequencies resonate with one another.

And here perhaps is a third function of the eyes, the ability to bring in the light of the higher consciousness; a form of light which we do not yet understand. Many of us know that it is there; others know but deny its existence and still others are completely unaware of its presence.

When we look at early pictures, particularly the early religious pictures, we may notice that practically every character has a halo of light around his head. They are not all saints by any means, although undoubtedly some of them are, but they are people who live in the higher consciousness. In such people, as in ourselves, this area of light which we now know as the aura is usually seen around the head. We have talked about this before and been shown how we may see it. We can also see in more highly evolved people that light is pouring down into the head and through the body. This is cosmic light, sustaining and energising the body in much the same way as light through the eyes.

We are literally 'garlanded in light' as well as being fed

and sustained by light – a light that shines in the darkness and the darkness comprehends it not.

In 1960, A B Lenner and others published a paper in *The Journal of Biological Chemistry* on the production of the hormone melatonin by the pineal gland.

The amino acid trytophan, from food, is converted from 5-hydroxytryptophan by an enzyme called tryptophan hydroxylase. The conversion requires a catalyst in the form of ferrous iron.

Following this the 5- hydroxytryptophan is converted into 5-hydroxytriptamine (now called serotonin). The enzyme causing this reaction requires a phosphorus containing chemical for its proper functioning.

Serotonin is not only confined to the pineal body but is found in other areas of the brain in high concentration. But in the pineal concentrations of serotonin undergo a rhythmic 24 hour cycle day/night. This is influenced by changes in light and darkness.

Serotonin is converted into melatonin by a transferase, an enzyme. Melatonin also has a 24 hour cycle which is influenced by alternate light and darkness.

The amount of light that we are exposed to seems to determine the amount of melatonin produced by the pineal gland. Light, therefore, is the controlling factor in the production of melatonin; it inhibits its formation. During the day the production of melatonin is low, at night in the dark it is higher. A dull or overcast day, a winter day without sun, and the levels of melatonin are high, a bright sunny day and they fall.

Which brings us to a condition rightly named SAD.

Seasonal Affective Disorder

Most people feel seasonal change. With the oncoming winter there is a general slowing down and lowering of mood and enthusiasm. But in those affected by SAD there are drastic mood swings and periods of serious debilitating depression. Unlike most people suffering from depression people with this disorder do not lose sleep and tend to eat more. Consequently they gain weight, they lose interest and become withdrawn. Some people undergo a change in personality. How many people? An estimated nearly 25 million in the USA. Four women to one man. It is a very common condition. And the treatment? Full-spectrum light… sunlight!

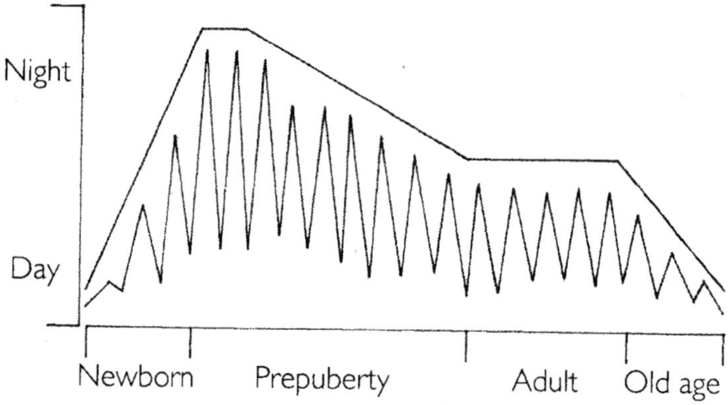

Melatonin rhythm

In 1815, J F Cauvin wrote:

> The influence of light on the morale of man is very powerful. The physician will prescribe sun for the sad and the weak. When taken with moderate exercise it

> will revive lost courage. The rich people of England and Germany go to the south of France and Italy to cure the disease of temper called spleen; or at least to get away from the monotony of an almost continuing climate.

So many people. I remember one of them, a friend. She was an artist. Strangely enough her paintings were all of light and darkness. As winter approached she gave up painting and went into hibernation in her little cottage on the moors. She did nothing. Ate, yes; slept, yes; all her creative talents were put to sleep. With the coming of spring the condition reversed and soon she was her old self, bright and shining and immensely creative. It was, she said, 'like coming out of hibernation!'

How can we help? We can trick the brain into thinking that it *is* spring! By artificial means of course. We can expose the affected person to artificial light.

The light must be bright. Sitting in a room with the light on is not enough. The brightness recommended is 2,500 lux. One lux is equivalent to one candle, one-fortieth the brightness of a sunny summer day. This seems to be enough and can be given by fluorescent light tubes in the correct amount. Coloured glasses are also of benefit. Red glasses seem to work best with autumn/winter depression.

18
Colour in Healing

The spectrum of light, visible and invisible, contains many frequencies. These we perceive as colour.

In the classical past, Pythagorus, Plato, Aristotle and Pliny considered the nature of colour and many of their views were held by the great painters, Leonardo da Vinci in particular.

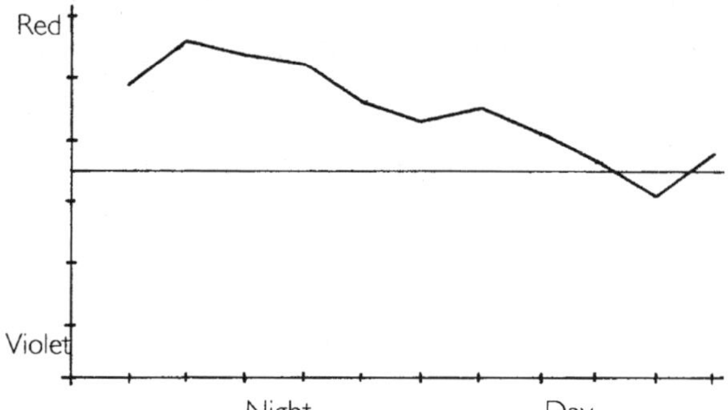

The effective colours inhibiting production of melatonin

Leonardo wrote:

> The first of all simple colours is white, though philosophers will not allow black and white to be colours, because the first is the cause or the receiver of colours, and the other totally deprived of them. White and black are doorways to spectrums, white contains all the colours in our spectrum, black goes into the spectrum. But as a painter cannot do without either, we shall place them among the others, and according to this order of things, white will be the first, yellow the second, green the third, blue the fourth, red the fifth and black the sixth. We shall set down white as the representative of light. White light is all encompassing without which no colour can be seen; green for the earth; blue for water; yellow for air; red for fire and black for total darkness – multidimensional or spatial.

He did not however attempt to organise colours any further and it was left to Sir Isaac Newton in the early 1670s to reveal that when white light is passed through a prism all the colours of the rainbow spring into being!

Nothing could have been more exciting than Newton's experiment. His finding revolutionised human thought on light and set into train all subsequent work in this area. A century later, primary colours of red, yellow and blue were described by J C le Blon and the colour circle was described by Morris Harris. His work and that of the many investigators who followed him was mainly concerned with the primary colours and their use in painting, and it was not until later that the nature of colour came under investigation. Much of this understanding came from Johann Wolfgang von Goethe, whom we know mainly as a poet and dramatist, but who was also an eminent scientist. It was Goethe who first noted that all colours came from black, moving from darkness into light, and Goethe who was deeply connected with its real nature. It was Goethe also who led Rudolph Steiner to experience and write about colour. From his work we learn that we must be able to experience colour or we cannot grasp what the world of colour is all about. We must in some way understand the effects of colour in the world in which we live, understanding that colour is energy and that the different colours are different levels of energy.

Remember the chakras!

As well as the levels of light that we can see and the colours that we see, the higher reaches of light are also open to us. The main route of entry of both higher and lower is the chakra system.

The colours within *white light* are vibrational energies, which are fundamental to the health and well being of the human form. Their action within the body is at cellular level and though most of the energy reaches the body through the eyes, the whole structure of our being senses colour and colour vibrations have their effect upon the body whether they are seen or not. Every cell within us can perceive the energies of colour because this is a wave pattern of energy that has within it a geometric structure. Its clarity affects the vibrancy of cellular encoding and where there is clarity of colour we find that the cellular encoding receives a pure note.

White light contains all the colours; perhaps this is what the body really needs? But if we sit in each colour separately we will notice that each one has a different effect on our body.

Below the red end of the colour spectrum in the area that our eyes cannot see is the colour of *infrared.* This is the thermal part of the light spectrum and we can feel it as heat. At the other end of the colour spectrum are the *ultracolours.* These colours cannot be seen by our eyes either and if used in healing may damage the eyes unless they are protected adequately by glasses. The colours at both ends of the spectrum may be used to heal, infrared specifically for inflammatory lesions and ultraviolet for skin conditions and general debility.

The individual colours that we are able to see have different properties and these are all used in healing.

Red light has the slowest wavelength and has also the greatest stimulating effect. It enters the body mainly at the sacral area and stimulates the cells of the adrenal gland to produce adrenaline. The circulating adrenaline acts on the heart muscle causing the heart to beat more rapidly and the blood pressure to rise. Circulatory deficiencies are helped. Sitting under a red light in a darkened room one can feel these things happening. But too much red can overstimulate and we can feel the other side of the picture: irritation and anger. For this reason when using red in healing it is important that we use it for a limited time only, preferably about ten minutes, then bringing in the complementary colour which in this case is turquoise. This prevents an overdose of the colour red.

Orange enters at the solar plexus. Being composed of red and yellow it has some of the characteristics of both colours. It also stimulates the adrenal glands; but it affects the thymus as well, probably because of the yellow component in the colour. Orange is a joyful colour and is not as heavy as red.

It is useful in infections and inflammatory conditions. Used with yellow it clears sluggish infections. The orange light stirs up the dormant state and the yellow helps the body to rid itself of the toxic wastes and generally tones up the system.

Green is a balancing colour, a harmonising colour. It soothes fretted nerves and as a nerve sedative it is of paramount value. It stimulates the heart gently and is anti-inflammatory to the tissues. It loosens and balances the etheric surround. One must be very careful in using green as a colour for healing because it can have a very deadening effect. Plants exposed only to green light die very quickly. Although one might say that almost everything in nature is green one must remember that the green used in healing is a flat uniform colour whereas the green of the trees and grass varies in shade and depth of colour, that there are other colours present and that there is movement as well as that indefinable essence, the energy that we call life.

We come now to the *higher colours*. These are vibrating much faster, entering through the higher centres of the body. Instead of being excitory they have a sedative action. *Blue light* will alleviate and remove pain. It has an antiseptic action. Entering at the throat level it has control over the thyroid gland, balancing the action. Blue soothes and restores calm and is useful in cases of mental overexcitement. It heals and strengthens the etheric body.

The blues which lie on either side of blue are *turquoise*, which has some of the properties of green, and *indigo*, which is a deep purplish blue. Indigo is a purifying colour which enters through the brow centre. We can use it on the eyes with beneficial effect but not for longer than about five minutes and never very close to the eyes as it may damage the retina. It has the effect of lengthening the sight. Indigo is also beneficial for glaucoma and cataract. It is of value in other conditions, for example in sinus trouble and facial paralysis. Here it is important that the eyes are covered.

Violet has many unknown qualities. Its functional frequency is attuned to the pineal gland and its main value as far as human illness is concerned is for mental and nervous disturbances. In violet the qualities of blue light are intensified and there is release of pain, sedation and antibacterial action. It should always be used with its complementary colour, *yellow*. If violet is given without the complementary the higher centres may be activated and psychic ability can develop rapidly. We cannot all cope with this.

All the colours are able to enter the body through the skin. Specific colours enter through individual chakra centres. The colour then acts upon the physical body in the area of the centre and affects the specific endocrine gland associated with the centre. Yellow entering at the splenic centre stimulates the pancreas; green, at the heart level, the thymus gland; blue at the throat chakra, the thyroid gland and so on. The effects will depend on the particular gland stimulated, the secretion of the gland affecting the body in its own specific way and not necessarily at the site of the gland which produces it. Thyroxin, for example, produced by the thyroid gland will have an effect on the total body metabolism, and the pancreatic secretion, insulin, controls blood sugar over the whole body.

How then should we use colour in healing? How can we prevent over stimulation of any one colour? Does the amount of colour needed vary from person to person?

All these questions will be discussed in the next chapter.

19
The Treatment of Illness by Colour

WHATEVER METHOD we may use to project colour, the choice of which colour to use is largely intuitive. It is not easy at first, but is essential if we are to be of any value to our patients.

So how do we start? I can only relate to my own experience and tell you what I do and what I feel when giving colour healing.

Before my patient comes, I meditate. Not for long, often for just a few minutes. In my meditation, I escape into a space where the hustle and bustle of everyday life cannot reach me – a quiet and peaceful haven, a holy place.

And now, refreshed and clear thinking, I wait for my client. The room is quiet, the light subdued, there is perhaps some music.

My patient arrives. He or she may be a complete stranger, or may be known to me. I may have been told the symptoms, I may be in the dark about the reasons for coming. We sit together and I encourage them to talk – to talk at first about anything they wish, gradually moving in conversation to the purpose of this visit. This is not a waste of time, for during this period I can feel the stresses and tensions within them and I start to understand their body's needs. Intuitively I begin to know which colours are the best to use.

I follow this with a healing period using my hands, moving down the chakra centres of the body: spiritual, mental, emotional and physical. Sometimes I can see the flow of colour; sometimes my patient will remark upon it. The healing finishes, what was necessary has happened, and we both return to the comfort of the little healing room.

There are, as always, variations upon this theme and no two healers will work in the same way. We all prefer to develop an individual approach to this very important field of therapy.

We may like to determine the colour that our patient needs by dowsing. This is another way of using our intuition; just as valid; just as effective. It is helpful to know before we dowse, a little about the condition of our client – not essential, but it helps. Then ask, 'what colour does X need?' We may be surprised at the answer!

Colours to use. We discussed the effects of the individual colours in the last chapter. Remembering that these are only guidelines, if our intuition suggests some other colour, something quite different, follow your intuition.

My early training as a colour therapist was at the Hygeia College of Colour Therapy, run by Theo Gimbel. After I had finished the course, I invested in his Colour Therapy Machine. This consisted of a rather unwieldy stack of boxes, each about the size of a small fridge. Each compartment had an electric light bulb in the back, and was fronted by a sliding glass panel of the appropriate colour, the main colour at the top of the machine and its complementary colour in the next section below. The treatment was timed; so many minutes for the main colour, so many minutes for its complementary colour. The times were determined by me by dowsing. I used this machine for several years and found it excellent for colour therapy. But it was rather cumbersome and I later began to treat my patients with a colour crystal torch with equally good results.

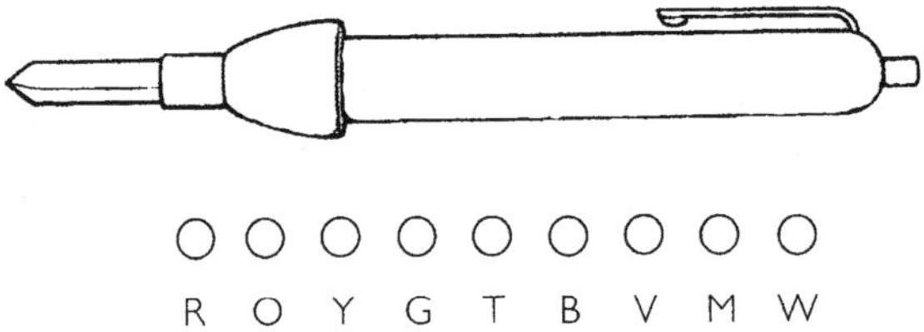

R Red
O Orange
Y Yellow
G Green
T Turquoise
B Blue
V Violet
M Magenta
W White

The Reflexology Crystal Torch

The torch was invented by Pauline Wills, a colour and reflexology therapist. Her work is described in *The Reflexology and Colour Therapy Workbook*, probably the best textbook for the would-be colour therapist. Pauline describes the crystal torch as follows: 'This instrument shines light through stained glass discs into a small single-terminated crystal. The crystal is set into copper in which a space is provided for the stained glass disc. Copper is related to the planet Venus, the planet of love; thereby, colour is brought into the crystal through the medium of love ... it contains the full vibrational spectrum of each colour. This enables the patient to absorb the exact shade that he or she needs.' Later in her book, she gives several pages of excellent guidelines showing the correct colours to use for the various bodily ills, a godsend to those who find the intuitive approach difficult, and something which is not possible to give in this textbook of healing.

There are many other ways to give colour to people: coloured clothing, coloured food, coloured drink. The latter can be given as solarised water. This is made by wrapping a sheet of coloured plastic around a bottle of spring water and standing the bottle in sunlight for several hours. The water is imprinted with the complementary of the colour used in the plastic.

Colour in the surroundings. Gone are the days when institutions; prisons, hospitals and schools were painted in good serviceable and hardwearing colours. Instead we meet all the colours of the rainbow and this is fine if several different colours are used in a ward or in a classroom. It is not so good though if the room in which we spend most of our time is painted in a single colour. Our needs vary, often from day to day. To use the colour *red*, for example in a working room such as a study could be a mistake. A red room has a contracting effect which is particularly so if the ceiling is also red. The effect of the colour is overstimulation and for anyone working there, particularly someone under stress, irritability and bad temper could be the result. In addition there might also be an increase of blood pressure.

Yellow is also a difficult colour to live with although we might consider it to be stimulating and cheerful. It has certain drawbacks as it is the colour of detachment. Entering through the lower splenic centre it affects the lower organs, stimulating them and purifying them. It increases the flow of vital fluids in the body and clears and clears sluggish conditions affecting the bowels and the bladder. It also acts on the central nervous system and to live in a yellow atmosphere could be detrimental to mental health. Yellow therefore should not be the only colour in a room, other than a toilet, but could be used for part of the room or for one wall.

Orange again is a stimulating colour. It has been said that orange is the colour of joy. A soft orange-pink stimulates in a higher sense than red and is at the same time warm, restful and without irritation. In all these colours if the complementary colour is used for furnishings or curtains the effect is heightened. Blue used with orange is an example of this.

There is some argument about the value of *green* in surroundings. Green is a balancing colour and as a wall covering it introduces stasis. In nature, green is the balanced state of being alive. As a decorative colour this is different. A room painted green becomes very static, very tiring and distressful. In an operating theatre, where green garments and towels are used frequently, the surgeon finds that he works at one speed, neither fast or slow. Not a bad thing really!

With *blue* and *violet* comes a feeling of calm and expansion. These colours are used extensively in decoration and furnishing. We must be careful where we use them because they can induce a pleasurable lethargy and as a result very little work is done. Violet does not have the same meaning to the wearer as it used to have, but its spiritual qualities are still associated with religion. We find the colour in funeral parlours where it gives the effect of spiritual calm, and in religious clothing where it confers dignity.

Magenta is the highest colour in the light spectrum. It is what is called an unsaturated colour, without the density of red and with the transparency of light. It is used sparingly in decoration but widely in the clothing industry. Rather strangely it has marked therapeutic qualities particularly for the hair, skin and nails.

Other colours are used in decoration, mixtures of one or more of the prime colours, such as *brown*. Brown is a sacrificial colour; the colour of dedication. If it is balanced with other colours that's fine, but by itself (brown panelling, brown carpet, brown furnishings) most people find it too heavy, except for those who are dedicated. So we have brown in the tax office, in Franciscan robes and, dare I say it, in the clothing of those dedicated ladies who do the flowers in church!

We come to *grey*; again a colour of denial much used in mourning. In the early part of the last century after the death of a loved one, ladies wore black for six months and then grey for the rest of their lives. It is a very depressing colour and should not be used in furnishings.

And *white*? White light contains all the colours and when used with coloured light can be effectively health giving. The effect of coloured light on white walls is to produce colour shadows, the shadow being the complementary colour of the lamp. A blue lamp, for instance will throw an orange shadow. Using coloured furnishings the room seems to become alive, harmonious, a delight to live and work in.

20
The Language of Colour

There are thousands of languages in the World, some clearly related, others, like the Basque language, seeming to have arisen from nowhere. All are different, and few people bother to learn more than one of them. We find it difficult to communicate with our neighbours in other countries. We tend to sound stupid and inarticulate and so, being British, we start to talk loudly in our own tongue, or to shout.

There is one language which can be understood by all; by plants, by animals, by insects and by humans, that hidden speech of nature, colour. We would do well to learn it. We need only to open our eyes or perhaps more importantly our understanding.

Colour! We see it with our eyes, but we can also 'see' with other parts of our body. Our skin for instance. One Russian woman could see colours through her skin to the degree that she could describe each one in detail. We also have this latent ability but it might take a lifetime to reach her perfection. If we are blindfolded and colour is played upon our skin, most of us with a little practice can determine from which end of the spectrum the colour comes. The denser slowly vibrating colours such as red and orange give us a feeling of contraction and the higher and faster vibrating colours of turquoise and blue a feeling of expansion and freedom. When the colour violet is projected the sensation is almost that of floating.

It would seem that as our brains develop further we will see a greater range of colour and this will probably extend into the higher ranges of the colour spectrum. Certainly this seems to have happened in the past. In 1880 Lazarus Geiger postulated that by examination of language, man appeared as little as 15,000 to 20,000 years ago to have perceived one colour only. He could not distinguish between the blue of the sky, the green of the grass and trees and the colour of the earth. This could, Geiger felt, be explained in terms of development of the eye and the brain. It is possible that at that time the centres in the brain dealing with colour had not yet developed fully or that the rod and cone mechanism of the eye was not sufficiently perfected. He based his observations on the primitive indo-european speech where there is no reference to colour in any form.

At a later period when the early Sanscrit writings, the Rig Veda, appeared, red, yellow and black were recognised as separate colours, to which was added white at a later date and eventually green. Blue seems not to have been recognised; in fact 'blue' is said to have been derived from a word that means black.

This was of course mainly speculation on the part of Geiger, but we can read in the Odyssey about the 'wine-dark sea' and the hair of Ulysses is described as 'hyacinth coloured'.

One would have thought that Homer, evolved as he was, would have seen colour much as we see it now. But Plato himself though experiencing blue says that it still has the colour characteristic of darkness. In the Bible most of the colours other than blue are mentioned frequently and blue is spoken of only occasionally and often in a context that shows that it was not recognised as a separate colour.

Once the great civilizations started to develop, we find that colour was used extensively and also ritualistically. The Chaldeans in Mesopotamia decorated their temples in the appropriate colours for the god who had his abode therein. In one temple dedicated to the planets, each planet was given a different colour. In Egypt temples and tombs were decorated internally with black, red, yellow, green, blue and purple. The gods and goddesses had special colours indicating their qualities. Osiris was often painted green because of his association with fertility. At certain festivals particular colours were used in ceremonial robes. Red was symbolic of life and victory and red and white together as in the flag of St.George expressed wholeness and perfection. White was the symbol of sacred things and of purity and sanctity.

Fashions and preferences change and evolve and in earlier times, warriors and peasants wore distinguishing colours. The Sumptuary Laws of the middle ages are an illustration of this. The laws not only regulated the richness and finery of the time but also the colours that might be worn by various levels of society. The peasants must wear drab browns, dull greens and greys, the more vivid colours being reserved for the higher orders. Heavy rich cloth and furs were forbidden to serf and peasant. Should a knight perceive that a man of the lower orders was wearing a fur collar on his garment he was entitled to rip it off.

> At the court of Richard II coats and hosen blazed with colour. The decent plain gown was abandoned for a short jacket and tight fitted hosen. One leg might be draped in red,the other in blue. Men 'wore their estates upon their backs', and flashed in jewels and costly stuffs no less than their wives. Youth was everywhere 'expressed in fancy'. Sleeves were slit to reveal more richness and shoes had points which were chained to the waist, 'preventing the wearer from saying his prayers' – *Trevelyan*

These laws were still in effect at the Renaissance but as the Black Death claimed the lives of thousands of peasants who formerly tilled the land, much of the countryside was turned over to sheep. The Guilds became more powerful and a wealthy middle class arose whose members began to wear the forbidden clothes and colours.

Although the Sumptuary Laws were no longer enforced, old customs die hard. We can still see the effects of repression of colour for the masses and the importance of its rentention in both Church and State. The Pope wears white; Cardinals, red; bishops purple; judges, red; kings and queens, purple; and the army has to be seen to be believed. Heads of State and self-proclaimed dictators wear all the colours of the rainbow because they are dimly aware that colour is important to their position, but are not quite sure how to handle the situation. More colours and more medals must mean a Superman!

In Victorian days the laws of colour in clothing were understood by all. Once again the poorer classes were uniformly drab and colour was only for their betters. Another pecking order, another time.

Enough of man! Rather sadly we have only aped the animals

and birds in our displays of brilliance. We can never excel the vivid display of the peacock, of the hummimg bird, of the baboon. But the language is the same; we know what is said and what is left unsaid in that unwritten tongue, the Language of Colour.

21
Sound

In the first book of the Jewish bible, which we now know as the Old Testament, we read:

> In the beginning was the Word and the Word was with God and the Word was God. All things were made by Him and without Him was not anything made.

The 'Word' that was God was in reality the sound of Creation, a sound of such high vibrational value that it does not lie within the range of the human ear, it lies beyond the frequency range of the dense form, that is to say, beyond human hearing. Sound then is the creator of form, the builder of the universe. Sound creates; but it can also destroy.

We can begin to understand the power of sound as a destructive, as well as a creative force when we remember that the high notes of the human voice can shatter glass. This is the negative aspect of the energy. On the positive, creative side, we must think of the many patterns and forms which we can see in the natural world around us. All, we are told, are the product of ultimate sound.

As the pure potential of creation, sound can be likened to the energies that are the basis of pure mathematics, beyond the understanding even of our most advanced physicists; although a breakthrough in their knowledge is imminent. Sound gives rise to the science of geometric form on all levels of vibration, and creates oscillations of energy that take wave form at lower frequencies, carrying the intelligence of the desired creation. On the planes or dimensions which vibrate at higher frequencies than the Earth, sound is the creator of Universal DNA. It affects the nature and balance of every cell in the human body and the cells also of animals and plants and other structures in the kingdoms of nature, notably crystals. Progress in understanding these areas has already begun and we are beginning to see that the results are of major importance to science.

The higher sound has frequencies and fluidity, an almost wave-like structure, and its frequencies are very specific according to the type of energy or sound being manifested. It can be varied with great precision depending on the desired result. In the lower frequencies of vibrational dimensions, it is a very tangible energy and one which we can experience for ourselves, varying as it does in pitch, in volume, and in tonal quality. Sound, at this level, the lower realms mirroring the higher, can be attractive, constructive, repellent or destructive; indeed it can be anything, for it is the energy of the creative process.

When the great stone circles were first built, the energies of sound were used to raise the stones. They were not put in place by man alone for he had not yet the ability to lift them. When the Pyramids took form, sound again may have been used as an energy in the lifting of the stones, and used also in many other great buildings. There is a story in the Far East concerning the raising of a great wall. It was composed of huge massive stones, much too heavy to lift. The priests and their acolytes stood before the stones, and behind the priests, the people. After the appropriate rites had been performed, the High Priest raised his arms, and the people sang one single note. One single clear note; and the stones, now light, were raised into place.

Many civilizations have moved and left no trace. Who knows how many times sound has been used as builder and creator? The echoes remain. We are told that the Earth was formed by sound, the so-called Big Bang theory. Whether this theory is true or not, we have no means of knowing. But there is historical evidence pointing to sound as a destroyer.

We read of Joshua, the son of Nun and the servant of his God, who walked with his people around the walls of Jericho for seven days and on the last day for seven times, and 'it came to pass at the seventh time when the priests blew on their trumpets before the Ark of the Lord, Joshua said to the people, "Shout!" And when the people shouted with a great shout, the walls fell flat and the people entered the city and utterly destroyed it'.

It would seem that Joshua himself wrote the description of that particular event. It filled nearly a chapter of the Jewish bible. We can be sure that he filled in the detail and that he wrote it for future generations to read. In this he was successful for we still sing of the time in the Negro spiritual of 'when the walls came tumbling down'.

The soprano sings a top note and shatters the glass chandelier. This has happened many times and the occasion has been recorded. How is this done? Almost certainly at the molecular level, the sudden burst of high energy disrupting the molecular structure of the glass. Sound can certainly destroy.

All manifested creation is organised and governed by one 'root' sound that permeates the entire universe and all that is within it. All of the energy of the Universe develops from this one sound and is in a continual state of transformation. At each succeeding moment the manifested universe continues to be created anew in response to the continuous root sound and this is the way that the manifested universe evolves from the unmanifested. All of manifest creation is in constant motion and the energy involved is never depleted. Everything that has become visible here on Earth has undergone a sort of contraction into visible form; into a liquid, a solid or a semi-solid. It is as if it were crystallised and it acts in a way that is governed by the laws of form. These laws date from the time of Pythagorus in 580-540 BC. They have of course existed for ever but they were first formulated by that great Initiate.

The five solids that Pythagorus described were used by Plato in his teachings in 375 BC and for this reason are called the Platonic Solids. They are the four-sided tetrahedron which we know as the pyramid, the six-sided hexahedron known as the cube, the octahedron which has eight sides, the twelve-sided dodecahedron and the twenty-sided icosahedron. Everything on Earth incorporates one or other of these structures. The structure is not always visible to the eye but the formulation or basis can be seen. The forms are present also in energy patterns and are symbolised in that branch of mathematics which we know as geometry. Mathematical order is present in all things, everything is interrelated and intercommunication between everything is possible. This is the message of Sacred Geometry where the laws apply not only to solids but also to angles and numbers.

You might think that the above would have little bearing on sound and healing but you would be wrong. The mathematics of the human body are vital to its performance. An example might be seen in the human body where the angle of the larynx in the female is 120 degrees, that of the male being 90 degrees. The wider angle allows the woman to be more intuitive; possibly the higher voice has bearing on this. Women who are particularly sensitive have an angle that is greater than 120 degrees.

The angle of the larynx determines the sound of the voice, or does the sound determine the angle of the larynx? Sound certainly seems to determine form and nowhere can this be seen more clearly than in the work of Dr Hans Jenny who observed and photographed the effects of sound upon matter.

He showed that if the spore powder of the Club Moss is spread evenly over a diaphragm and the diaphragm is vibrated by sound waves produced vocally or by a musical instrument, a galaxy of little piles of powder is formed. Each pile rotates on its own axis and also rotates as a single body rather as in our own solar system. Patterns are formed which become more and more elaborate as the pitch of the note rises. Apparent chaos is resolved into order. Similarly when liquids are made to vibrate in the same way, very unusual patterns develop, in particular a cellular pattern, not unlike those that are found in the natural world. When the materials and frequencies of sound are changed, beautiful structural patterns are released, hexagonal and regular arrangements like honeycomb or lattice networks. Sometimes the texture of the material used undergoes a marked change so that once the vibration has ceased we have a different substance, a different type of matter.

This branch of natural science is called cymatics. It is the study of the effect of sound upon matter, the proof that sound is able to change form.

A Chladni Image from the work of Hans Jenny

Substance is the potential state in the Universe and is similar to a chemical in solution just before precipitation. Matter is the precipitate. In the cosmos, sound moving in orderly sequence causes substance to precipitate and it becomes matter, becomes structured, becomes the Universe as we know it.

Einstein regarded the underlying field out of which matter was precipitated as the ultimate physical entity, a continuous medium which is present everywhere in space. He regarded particles or forms as local condensations of the field in areas where the field is very intense. He saw no place for matter as a separate entity and felt that the field was the only separate reality. We do not know whether Einstein considered this quantum field as a field of cosmic sound.

Once the substance has been precipitated, what then? Does sound have any further bearing on the form? To answer this, let us look within the dimensions of our world and try to see the effect of sound on matter which is already there.

For this we must move into the realm of music and look at the effect that music has on form.

In music when a single note is produced this is called a fundamental. Other notes also sound and these are in mathematical relationship to the first note. These are the harmonics or overtones. The first harmonic which is sounded vibrates twice as fast as the first note, the second three times as fast, the third four times as fast, and so on. It is possible to set in resonance and in entrainment, frequencies which may be lower or higher than our first sound. Sounds which we normally cannot hear, such as the deep sound of the Earth Note can become audible. Through this principle of correspondence, we are able to use harmonically related sounds to influence the atomic structure of crystals or plant and animal structure.

The principle of resonance is used in industry to convert sound into light. Different crystals can resonate and amplify different harmonics. The quartz crystal is a good example. The quartz crystal is an oscillator. It can be cut to a specific configuration and tuned by pressure. In this way it produces sound which is subsonic and which in turn produces luminescence. Sound then can generate light.

22
Natural Sound

Peter Tomkins and Christopher Bird are co-authors of two remarkable books, *The Life of Plants* and *Secrets of the Soil.* They are both leading experts in the field of the natural world. Writing about the effects of sound on plant energies, they state that plant life flourishes when certain music is played. Seeds germinate more quickly and sprout faster. More crops are produced when continuous tones of a certain pitch are played. Conversely, random noise and certain notes can retard the growth of plants and even kill them.

Further observations have been made by Dorothy Retaliak, an American botanist who, when working for her PhD. thesis, subjected plants to different types of music. She found that when Indian sitar music was played to plants, they leaned towards the source of the sound. They reacted in the same way to Western classical music. The plants remained indifferent to country and western music and to composers such as Schoenberg. But, if percussive drum music were played, and in particular hard rock music, the plants leaned away as far as they were able. One could hardly blame them.

Shakespeare writes;

> Orpheus with his lute made trees
> And the mountain tops that freeze
> Bow themselves when he did sing:
> To his music plants and flowers
> Ever sprung, as sun and showers
> There had made a lasting Spring.

Dorothy Retaliak was not the first to observe the phenomenon!

Some members of the animal world have better hearing than man and may be able to hear supersonic sound. Dolphins and whales are particularly sensitive to sound. Their hearing is very acute and extends far beyond the human range. Sound travels four times as fast in water as in air. Many members of the whale family, the cetacea, do their hunting by sonar or echo soundings. The dolphin sends out sonic or supersonic clicks in bursts of up to 800/second. The sonic information seems to be received by the forehead, which in the dolphin and more particularly in the sperm whale acts as an echo-locating organ, giving directional information. The whale can then tell the distance, shape, size and species of other animals and fish. The echo is heard with the pitch change of a Doppler effect, the pitch rising as the object draws nearer and falling away as it moves away. The distances are perceived as different rhythmic intervals.

The humpback whale produces musical sounds. The song of the whale in the Atlantic Ocean is different from that of whales living in the Pacific, although both groups of whales have phrases in common. The humpback whales sing a different song each year and the same song travels over distances of many miles.

Sound also has a high level of importance in land animals, not only between animals of the same species, but also between animals of different species, a prime example of this being the communication between animals and man. The sounds used in communication of this sort are termed speech. Speech seems to be able to alter and transform in some way both animals and man. It has a soothing effect when we speak softly and the reverse when we speak in anger.

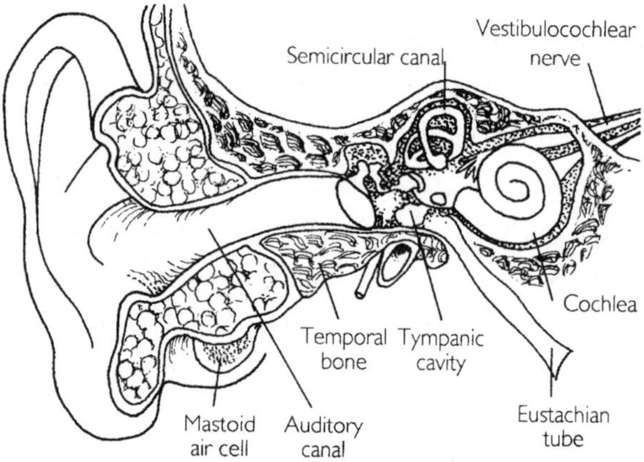

Structure of the ear

Sound enters the body through the ear and vibrates the eardrum. Bone is a prime conductor of sound and the energy is transmitted through a chain of tiny bones to the inner ear. Sound is now a physical vibration. The vibrations next reach the cochlea, a snail-shaped organ lying in the area behind the eye. The cochlea is fluid filled and inside its coiled length has little hair-like structures. The hairs in the cochlea are the means by which the physical vibrations of sound are conveyed to the auditory pathways of the brain. They are essential to hearing and are easily destroyed by loud noise, in particular the heavy beat of modern music. Once destroyed they do not reform and the individual becomes deaf.

Auditory pathways from the ear enter the brain through the medulla oblongata and the sensory data is 'sifted' by a system known as the Reticular Activating System before it proceeds via the thalamus to the auditory area of the cerebral cortex. The sifting either alerts or sedates the neocortex and by this means affects the bodily function. Sound which comforts and soothes by its rhythm, melody or harmonics is thought to reduce stress levels. It lowers the rate of respiration and heart contraction.

What mother does not talk to her baby, sing to her baby? No harsh notes are involved. The voice is gentle and the harmonic frequencies are in the higher frequency bands. This is the medium for normal and natural growth. But if loud noises are heard, the parents perhaps are quarrelling, the child may stop listening or, worse still, the organs within the child's body may be affected in development. Much of the normal growth may be retarded and perhaps it is at this time that the seeds of much future illness are sown. In the light of these observations, an interesting study was made of premature babies. A group of premature babies was divided. One half of the group was placed in an area where the Brahms Lullaby was played quietly on a loop tape for some hours each day, and the other half was kept in a room without music. The 'Brahms' babies were more relaxed, cried less, put on weight and were able to leave the hospital a week earlier than the control group.

Speech facilitates communication and cognitive ability but may also have unanticipated effects in human beings. Some neurophysiologists have hypothesised that vocal vibration associated with human use of language causes a kind of cleansing of the cerebrospinal fluid. It has been observed that vibrations may precipitate and concentrate small molecules in the spinal fluid which bathes and continuously purifies the brain. Our ancestors may have, consciously or unconsciously, discovered that vocal sound cleared the chemical cobwebs out of their heads. This may have brought about the evolution of our present-day thin skull as opposed to the larger and thicker skull of prehistoric man and as an added bonus, our desire to communicate by words. From this it follows that a process as simple as talking or singing might make the removal of chemical waste from the brain more effective.

> Vibrations of the human skull such as produced by loud singing or vocalisation exert a massaging effect on the brain and facilitate elution of metabolic products from the brain into the spinal fluid. The Neanderthals had a brain fifteen per cent larger than we have and yet they did not survive in competition with more modern humans. We think that their brains were more polluted because their massively thick skulls did not vibrate and therefore the brain was not sufficiently cleaned. In the evolution of modern humans the thinning of the cranial bones was important. Changes in diet from specialised and limited, to omnivorous, refined and narrowed the jaw and modified the muscles of the face and throat, facilitating the development of articulation. (*K F and H Tindrak*)

Speech seems to have facilitated communication and cognitive ability in this way.

This was an important step forward for man.

We probably know more about the effects of sound upon the human body than we do about its effects on other animals, although most of our knowledge and understanding in this area applies equally to the animal form in general.

Cells within the body are constantly moving and the movement causes friction and creates sound, in the form of a single note. Tunes are to be found in body chemistry! Aminoacids, for example are made up of atoms, basic elementary particles, which when grouped together in compound form produce frequencies of sound which in turn create a melody. In a similar way, each organ has its own group of sounds, its own melody, its own song. In very truth the heart sings and the whole body can itself be a symphony.

Olivea Dewhurst-Maddock in *The Book of Sound Therapy* writes: 'composers of music can reflect their own bodily balance in their work, by choosing intuitively the tunes within them which are connected to their own rhythm and produced by their cells'. Their music may reflect their own health or illness, and I feel that this might apply to Tchaikowsky in particular. No-one who has listened to his sixth symphony, the 'Pathetique', can doubt his mental anguish when he was writing the music. Perhaps we tend to understand the music of a composer more in terms of mental health than physical but physical illness can also be detected in the music of a composer. In this context we can include Beethoven, who was eventually completely deaf. It has been said that some of the music of J S Bach is so close to the sound of the digestive tract that he may have had trouble in this area!

Sound influences life patterns, not only the physical patterns but mental and emotional states. Live sound contains harmonics and overtones but recorded sound does not have these and those people who do not experience live sound may be unable to bring in harmony at cell level.

Cyril Scott, the pianist, says that the great collective movements of the human soul have always been anticipated by innovations in music. In the world of great classical music, Handel's Oratorios acted as a brake on the licentious tendencies of eighteenth century England. The music of Chopin awakened a new desire for culture. That of Schubert and Mendelsohn preceded a time of social change which led to the abolition of child labour and of slavery in the West.

It would seem then that the music which is written and performed may determine the way that society will develop. A great deal of the unrest and unease that we are experiencing now may be associated with heavy beat music, particularly when played with strobe lighting.

Dr Peter Guy Manners, who is a pioneer in the study of the effects of harmonic frequencies on the body, says:

> A healthy organ will have all its molecules working together in harmonious relationship with each other and they will all be of the same pattern. If different patterns enter the organ the harmonious relationship could be upset. If these frequencies are weak in their vibration they will be overcome by the stronger frequencies of the native ones. If, on the other hand, the foreign vibrations prove to be the stronger, they may establish their disharmonious pattern in the organ or in other tissues, and this is what we call disease.

> If a treatment contains a harmonic frequency pattern which will reinforce the organ or the organs affected, the vibrations of the intruder will be neutralised and the correct pattern for the organ re-established. This should be a curative reaction.

Manners used radionic frequencies to bring the correct harmonic frequencies into the different areas of the body.

The most perfect way to introduce healing into the body is through the human voice. The pioneer in this field is Sharry Edwards. More than twenty years ago, during an acoustic test, she found that she has extremely acute hearing, which is well beyond the normal range of 20,000 cycles per second and that she also has an exceptional voice and can duplicate pure tones with precision. Later she found that the sounds which she was hearing and duplicating could be related to musical notes that were in 'stress' in a persons speaking voice. By stress is meant that the notes were missing or out of tune, as indeed were the people themselves. Giving these people back the pure note that was stressed in their speaking voice changed their brain frequencies and restored their good health.

Bioacoustics is the name given to the study of the effects of sound on the human body. Though still in its infancy it may prove to be the healing of the future. The basis of this type of treatment is the resonance or vibratory frequency of the part affected. If this part of the body becomes diseased, the resonance alters, but we are now able to project the correct frequency into the area affected and return it to its normal state.

Ideally the natural voice should be used in treatment, but few practitioners have sufficiently pure tone and recordings of the voice or of musical instruments are usually employed.

Using the western chromatic scale the rates created from the first seven harmonics can be used to resonate the chakras. There is a definite relationship between the pitch of the note used and the individual chakra. The second to the eighth harmonics respectively resonate, the base chakra resonating with the second harmonic rising to the crown resonating with the eighth. The body cells are able to select the frequencies that they need for health from those that are presented to them.

We have stressed repeatedly that sound can both destroy and create form and this is equally true whether the form is a part of the universe or the cells of the body. In my understanding, each cell or group of cells has its own note, its own frequency or range of sounds to which it responds. Rather like the bar code at a supermarket we carry in our make-up a range of frequencies which are essentially our own. As individual as a fingerprint, this is our own signature sound. If the pattern is altered in any way, our body cells may become affected, so much so that they may take up a new way of growth, they may in fact become a cancer. Alternatively they may die.

Can we reverse this? In theory the answer is, Yes! In practice the pattern is more difficult to reverse. The cell will however accept the level of sound that it needs for health, provided that level is presented to it and that the sound is not blocked out by dissonance.

The human voice can carry the frequencies that are needed. Few of us have perfect pitch but the body cells are able to select the frequencies that they need for health, disregarding those that they do not need.

Music can heal, baroque and classical music, the music of some of our greatest composers; and if possible we should listen to live music, instrumental music. Like plants the body may respond best to the sitar! Music making in itself is a form of therapeutic activity, a source of deep satisfaction, a healing process.

And natural sound, the fluid sounds of bird song, the sound of the running stream, the wind in the trees; all these can heal. Try them! Try also the sound of silence and the healing of sound outside audible range, the sound beyond sound, the voice of God.

FINALE

'Thou shalt not kill, but needst not strive
officiously to keep alive.'
– A H Clough, *The Latest Decalogue*

SHOULD WE ATTEMPT to heal everyone? Whether they wish it or not?

Sometimes, it seems, natural death is the great healer.

Margaret was my neighbour and my friend. She lived in the row of cottages across the road. Solid, dependable, safe, that was Margaret.

As she became older, she began to disintegrate mentally. This took a strange form and she found it very worrying. An imaginary family moved into her cottage: a married couple, their child and the mother-in-law. Margaret was not quite sure where this elderly woman fitted in, but she found her very frightening.

The situation deteriorated during the following months. The child was forever playing in the road. 'She'll be run over', said Margaret. Her mother monopolised the little gas stove: cooking – always cooking; and the man: 'He never moves, he just stands there at the foot of the stairs and watches me. Sometimes he looks like a coat, sometimes like something else.' The mother-in-law? 'She's in my bed,' said Margaret, 'takes her knickers off.'

'But where do you sleep?'

'I sleep in my chair.'

The weeks passed. Margaret was now physically ill and was moved to the local old folks home. I went to see her. Sitting there, oblivious to the babbles and shrieks of those around her and to the sweet stench of urine, she radiated happiness. She died a few days later, free at last.

I wrote this poem for her:

For Margaret
Margaret sits in her wheelchair,
Quietly dementing
 And happy as a sandlark.
She has, she tells me,
Just returned from Devon;
Or was it Cornwall,
Yes, Land's End.
She's been to see a friend
Working in the saltmines.
And did I know
That salt is mixed with silver?
Fancy that!
But on the other hand,
When salt is mixed with sand – it often is –
It eats your money up,
Even within your hand.

And, à propos of nothing,
Did I know
That tiny crocodiles are bred
To nibble at the feet
Of the elite?
That's what she said.
And then she fell asleep
Like a small baby
Newly born.
I felt I could not weep.

BIBLIOGRAPHY

Bachler K *Earth Radiation: Startling Discoveries of a Dowser* (Wordmasters 1988)

Bird C *The Divining Hand* (Whitford Press 1993)

Bird C and Tomkins P *Secrets of the Soil* (Earthpulse Press 1998)

Bird C and Tomkins P *The Secret Life of Plants* (Arkana 1991)

Burr Professor H *Blueprint for Immortality* (C W Daniel 1972)

Dewhurst-Maddock O *The Book of Sound Therapy* (Gaia Books 1993)

Goldman J *Healing Sounds. The Power of Harmonics* (Element Books 1996)

Jenny H *Cymatics Vols 1 & 2* (Basilius Press 1967)

Liberman J *Light, Medicine of the Future* (Bear & Co 1992)

Manners P J *Cymatics*

Nieper Dr. H *Revolution in Technology, Medicine and Society*

Ott J N 'Colour and Light: their effects upon plants, animals and people' (J. Biosocial Research 7, Part 1 (1985))

Raphaell K *Crystal Enlightenment* (Aurora 1991)

Roeder D *The Sound of Music and Plants* (De Vorss)

Steiner R *Colour* (Rudolf Steiner Press 1997)

Tomatis A *The Conscious Ear* (Station Hill Press 1991)

Tomkins P *The Secret Life of Nature* (HarperCollins 1998)

Wills P *The Reflexology and Colour Therapy Workbook* (Element Books)

Carol Brierly was born near Harrogate at the end of the 1914–18 war while her father was still in France. One of five children, her early life was rich in the freedom that helped develop her individualistic character.

From the age of eight she experienced severe illness. Because of this she was not expected to excel in the academic field. In the middle of a course at technical college on cooking and sewing, she decided to become a doctor and switched courses. She qualified from the University of Leeds Medical School in 1949.

Throughout her life she has learnt to cope with many hardships. She understands only too well the pain, frustration, deep unhappiness and fear experienced by patients; she also knows how to deal with these emotions from deep within.

After her retirement as a consultant dermatologist, she founded the Prometheus School of Healing near Huddersfield, which ran until the early nineties.

She has a diploma from the White Lodge School of Psychotherapy, and an honorary doctorate from the Open International University for Complementary Medicine. She has lectured in the UK and Europe on alternative healing and related spiritual subjects. She was for two years President of the World Federation of Healing.